Caring for Older People

D1426235

This book is dedicated to the memory of my grandmother

Beatrice Louise Sykes.

THE LIBRARY
GUILDFORD COLLEGE
of Further and Higher Education

Caring for Older People

Jacci Stoyle
RGN Cert. Ed.

WITHDRAWN

Stanley Thornes (Publishers) Ltd

Text © Jacci Stoyle 1991
Original line illustrations © Stanley Thornes (Publishers) Ltd 1991

All rights reserved. No part of this publication may be reproduced or transmitted in any form or by any means, electronic or mechanical, including photocopy, recording or any information storage and retrieval system, without permission in writing from the publisher or under licence from the Copyright Licensing Agency Limited. Further details of such licences (for reprographic reproduction) may be obtained from the Copyright Licensing Agency Limited, of 90 Tottenham Court Road, London W1P 9HE.

First published in 1991 by:
Stanley Thornes (Publishers) Ltd
Ellenborough House
Wellington Street
CHELTENHAM GL50 1YD
England

Reprinted 1993
Reprinted 1994

362.6
STO

77349

British Library Cataloguing-in-Publication Data

Stoyle, Jacci
    Caring for older people.
    I. Title
    362.607

    ISBN 0–7487–0451–5

Figurative illustrations by Robin Wiggins
Diagrams by Chris Lyon
Typeset by Tech-Set, Gateshead, Tyne & Wear
Printed and bound in Great Britain at Redwood Books, Trowbridge, Wiltshire

Contents

Acknowledgements

This book could never have been written without the help, support and knowledge of a great many people. I have approached older people, care workers, colleagues, students, voluntary organisations and community representatives for information. It has been an uplifting experience to find so many people willing to offer their time and indeed themselves to enable me to write this book.

I cannot mention everyone individually but I should like to say a special thank you to those people who have given me tremendous support, and to all those people in Age Concern who gave me a wealth of information on a variety of projects concerned with ethnic elders.

Thank you Leslie Heslop and Naheed Hussain for the interesting and personal insights into your cultural values which you both gave me. Also to Rhona Alekna and Jean Lucas for their contribution to nursing people of different cultural backgrounds.

Two people have encouraged me along the way, offering enormous support with time, information, resources and ideas. I should like to say a special thank you to Eric Pemberton for extending his incredible network of contacts and resources to help me and to Sue Knottenbelt for her proofreading and her honesty.

Finally I should like to give my thanks to two other people who have made sacrifices so that this book could be written. Thank you Andrew and Jacob Stoyle for the endless cups of tea, your expertise with the word processor and your unflagging support.

Jacci Stoyle
1991

Introduction

TRAINING FOR CARE

There is a wide range of jobs in caring for older people. Some of these are professional positions which require a high level of training to degree standard and beyond. At one time almost the only route to these professional qualifications was through GCSE equivalents and A levels.

More recently other vocational qualifications have been created to cater for the pre-professional levels of caring. These are recognised in their own right, as well as offering people of all ages alternative routes through to higher qualifications and professional status. Colleges of Further Education offer a range of BTEC and City and Guilds courses which often operate on a flexible part-time basis, to enable people with domestic and working commitments to attend.

Polytechnics and other institutions involved with health or learning programmes can sometimes offer short courses to update skills or to provide useful additional skills. For example, St John's Ambulance run a variety of courses in First Aid and Caring for the Sick.

From 1992 all existing vocational qualifications will have an additional NVQ (National Vocational Qualification) level of 1, 2, 3 or 4. These are four pre-professional levels of competence indicating to an employer a person's ability to do particular areas of work. This has been accomplished in order to standardise the variety of different qualifications available, so that both employers and students can better understand their worth and their parity with each other.

All carers should try to take the opportunities available for learning, whether they are paid or unpaid practitioners, family members, or professionals keeping up with the latest developments. Sometimes it is easy to pick up bad habits of practice when you are working in a busy situation; the wide range of courses and seminars available offer carers the opportunity to reflect on their own practice and to discuss common difficulties with other experienced colleagues. As the carer's range of knowledge and skills increases, they can develop personally as well as professionally, which is beneficial both to clients and to carers themselves.

It is perhaps hardest for relatives struggling to cope with an infirm elderly person to see how they could spare the time or the money for a luxury such as a course in caring. However, the benefits for such people would be tremendous. They would have a forum for sharing anxieties and an opportunity perhaps to discover resources, services, benefits, techniques or time-savers which could help them. They might also find the break away from home and the company of others with similar interests and problems both practically and emotionally supportive.

Often courses are very cheap to people on low incomes and are offered at flexible times. Local health clinics sometimes run courses for home carers and support or self-help groups can arrange to have a speaker at one of their meetings. Caring for Carers is an organisation which provides support to relatives caring for older people. They may be able to advise carers on local ventures, groups or schemes.

REFERENCES TO OLDER PEOPLE

The terms older people and elders are used interchangeably throughout this book to describe those people who are more usually referred to as 'the elderly' or 'the aged'. The terms 'elderly' or 'aged' can appear to group all older adults together, preventing people from remembering that they are individuals who happen to be old. Older people must be considered in the same way we would consider all adults, with the right to make decisions, follow the cultural values of their choice and to retain dignity and independence.

The term 'elder' is used in the Afro-Caribbean culture to describe older people. It has been used throughout the book to show the importance of considering the differences between cultural norms and working to recognise them in order to care for all people as they would wish to be cared for.

MEDICAL TERMS

The reader may not be familiar with all of the medical terms used in the text. The words and phrases set in **bold type** are explained in The Glossary of Medical Terms, pages 147–8.

Carers and the Cared For

WHO ARE 'OLDER PEOPLE'?

The following case studies look at some older people living in Britain today.

CASE STUDY *Hyacinth Taylor*

Hyacinth Taylor is a 70-year-old Afro-Caribbean woman who lives with her husband in Handsworth, Birmingham. They own a terraced house with a small back yard, which is filled with tubs of colourful flowers. This is what she has to say about her life today.

'I lead a busy life, you know. My husband and I are lucky that we've still got our health. We get involved with the Church a lot, not just Sundays, we always go Sunday evenin', I love to sing, you know. We often help out with the different social activities; I go down to the Day Centre and do the teas and sometimes help with the Luncheon Club. I visit a sister* in her home, who is stuck in all day after her stroke. My daughter laughs at me; she says I should be takin' it easy at my age an' folks should be visitin' me.'

*Members of the congregation at Hyacinth's Church always refer to each other as brothers and sisters.

CASE STUDY *Alex Evans*

Alex Evans is an 82-year-old widower who lives in the heart of the Devonshire countryside on the edge of Dartmoor. He has been a farmer all his life and still helps out on the farm where he lives with his son and daughter-in-law. His grandson still lives at home and also runs the farm.

'Farming is my life – I couldn't imagine doing anything else. Every morning I still like to get up early to help with the milking, it's the best time of the day. I've got a marvellous vegetable garden which is my pride and joy. I potter about there most afternoons; there's always something to do in a garden. It's been been a solace for me since I lost the wife. Of course I can't do the same on the farm as I could do when I was a younger man but I'm still a useful pair of hands. Fresh air and plenty of hard work have kept me as fit as a fiddle.'

CASE STUDY   *Alicia Williams*

Alicia Williams is a Polish woman who came to this country during the war and married an English man. She is 76 years old and lives with her husband in a semi-detached house in the suburbs of Manchester.

'I am lucky to have had a very happy marriage. My husband and I share so much together. We were not blessed with children and perhaps that is why we are so close now. We haven't a lot of money but with the concessions and discounts available for pensioners we manage to go out several times a week. We play golf at the municipal course, go swimming and belong to the local rambling club.

We have all the time in the world for each other now that we have retired' and it's like a second honeymoon. I love young people but they make me smile – they think sex is just for them – it's not of course!'

Any book which seeks to offer advice on caring for a particular client group will, of necessity, focus on the difficulties that are likely to occur in order to prepare and aid the reader in facing those difficulties. If this were a book about the care of children then the various problems discussed would be balanced by the reader's and the author's pleasure at the prospect of watching a young person grow and develop, gaining greater independence every day. Unfortunately the benefits of growing old are not so easily demonstrated. It is therefore useful to introduce these three older people, who are living such full and purposeful lives, as indeed many elders do. As we shall be exploring the circumstances of less fortunate elders, who are often dependent on others, it is important to keep a sense of proportion and not to imagine that all older people need care.

DEFINING OLD AGE

Concepts of ageing vary from person to person and are influenced by personal experience, role models, the media and the attitudes of the cultural background and society in which we live. Often old age is used to describe someone's condition or behaviour rather than the number of years they have lived. For example, we might say of a previously active 80-year-old person: 'Elsie's really aged since she went into hospital. She can't walk without help and she's become very confused.' Elsie may still be 80 years old so she has not aged more than a few weeks; what is meant is that she has become closer to the image which the speaker has of being old. We shall be examining attitudes to ageing, and to older people in general, later in the chapter.

Older people are usually defined as those who are over the official age of retirement, which is presently 60 years old for women and 65 years old for men. The age at which people retire from certain jobs has become flexible in recent years and the official age of retirement is likely to be the subject of legislational change. Some people retire early, at 50, for example, and others continue to work past their 65th birthday. Sometimes people become disabled in their fifties and enter residential accommodation for older people before they are 60 years old.

For the purposes of this book references to older people will be, generally speaking, to those who are 60 years old and over. This is meant as a guide to the reader and is not an absolute rule. This age group includes people who may be 100 years old or more, so there is an age span of at least 40 years. Forty years spans two generations of people with different life experiences, which have shaped their attitudes and values. Therefore a further distinction may be made, to help carers of older people. For the purposes of statistics, older adults are defined as being 'young old' and 'old old'. 'Young old' people are aged from 60–75 years old and the 'old old' are 75 years old and over.

Care should be taken not to stereotype older adults in these two categories but, as you will see, there are differences between the two groups which can guide you as a carer.

POPULATION TRENDS

Although the number of elders in the population has stabilised, the proportion of very old people has continued to increase due to the baby boom at the turn of the twentieth

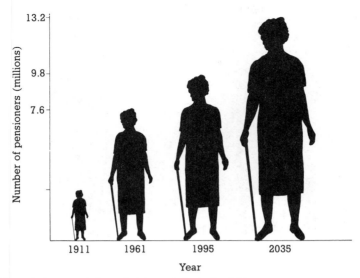

Figure 1.1   *Trends in population of older adults in the UK*

century (see Figure 1.1). Improvements in public health care towards the end of the nineteenth century meant that more children were surviving in Victorian times than had previously been the case. The younger old people were born a generation later. The birth rate dropped from the period following the First World War till the 1930s. Many women from the Victorian baby boom did not marry because of a shortage of men, resulting from the losses in the First World War and the number who emigrated to the New Commonwealth to find employment. Family planning was possible at this time for those who did marry and one or two children became a more popular family size. Abrams (1978) claims that 30 per cent of women had no children and 45 per cent had only one or two. This is important to remember as it means that many of our frail and vulnerable very old members of society will have no children to support them now.

The following facts and figures describe the nature and circumstances of the older population in the UK today.

- People aged 75 and over are less likely to be living in a family. Five per cent of men and 24 per cent of women in the 'younger old' group live alone, whereas 7 per cent of men and 40 per cent of women in the 'older old' group live alone.
- People from the 'old old' age group are more likely to be poorest due to using up their savings. They are less likely to have private pension schemes or to own their homes. Their accommodation will be older and in greater need of repair and they are less likely to have adequate heating or inside toilets.
- Two-thirds of pensioners are women, but the ratio of women to men increases by four to one in the case of elders over the age of 85. (See Figure 1.2.) This is

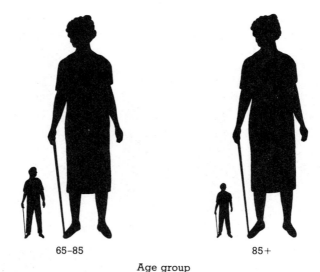

65–85   85+

Age group

Figure 1.2   *The ratio of men to women in older age groups*

because women live longer than men and, as mentioned earlier, many men died
in the First World War or emigrated to find work.
- Six per cent of people over 60 years old are in some form of residential care;
  3 per cent of people aged 60–75 years are in residential care and 21 per cent of
  those aged 75 and over are in residential care.
- Nineteen per cent of the population are over 65; 3 per cent of these are from the
  New Commonwealth and Southern Asia.

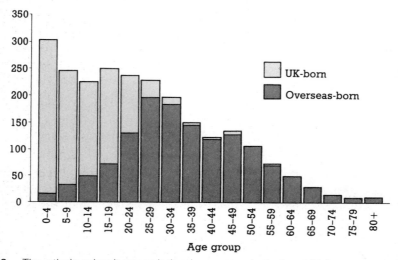

Figure 1.3   *The ethnic minority population by age and whether UK-born or overseas-born,
1984–86 average*

Source: *Social Trends 19*, © Crown copyright 1989. Reproduced courtesy of HMSO

- Although the number of ethnic elders is still small compared to the total population of elders, the proportion is increasing due to the fact that the people who came to this country in the 1950s are now approaching their old age. The majority live in inner city areas, forming a large proportion of that elderly population. Figure 1.3 illustrates the increasing number of ethnic elders amongst the older population, and the fact that most of them have been born overseas. The implications of caring for this group will be discussed throughout this book.

WHERE ARE OLDER ADULTS FOUND?

The following illustrations show some of the situations and settings in which older people may be found.

A nursing home

Photograph courtesy of Marie Curie Cancer Care

A residential home

Photograph courtesy of McCarthy & Stone

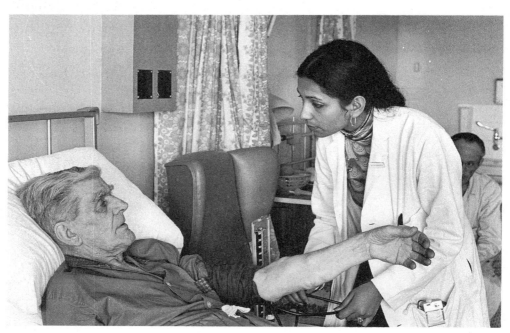

A hospital ward

Photograph courtesy of Age Concern, © Sally and Richard Greenhill

Sheltered housing

Photograph courtesy of McCarthy & Stone

They may be living:

- in a rural community
- in a suburb or an inner city area
- in residential accommodation
- with a son or daughter and family
- in sheltered accommodation
- in a long stay or temporary hospital
- with a partner, or a brother or sister of similar age
- in a nursing home
- with foster carers in their own home.

In some of these situations elders require different amounts of care. Before looking at who provides that care it is necessary to consider what is meant by caring.

DEFINING CARING

ACTIVITY

1 Think hard about what caring means to you. You have been cared for at some time in your life, for example, when you were a baby and when you were at school, by a teacher or a friend. You may have cared for others at some time; perhaps you brought someone a cup of tea when they were not feeling well or did the shopping for a frail neighbour or relative.

Write down all the different aspects of caring that you can think of – the small things as well as the big things, as they are all important. It is helpful to do this sort of exercise with a colleague or friend, as often other people's ideas can further stimulate your own.

Here are a few suggestions to start you off:

Caring is . . .

- looking after somebody when they are ill
- being nice to mum when she is tired
- helping someone to the toilet
- listening to someone's troubles.

2 Look at your list and consider whether some of the aspects which you wrote down involve feelings, such as being sympathetic; whether some involve actions, such as helping a person into bed; or whether any involve taking responsibility, such as being reliable or punctual? Discuss your list with some other people.

Caring is a combination of putting into practice feelings and actions and using knowledge and skills to allow someone else to live as independently as possible, in the way they would choose to do if they were able.

Caring can be done badly and it can be done well. You may know the difference yourself if you have ever needed caring for and remember the experience. Good caring requires an imaginative approach; carers need to imagine what it must be like to be the client. They must be able to listen properly so that they provide what people really want. Listening is a crucial part of verbal and non-verbal communication and is a highly skilled technique.

The caring role is explored in more detail in the following pages. First it is necessary to look at who the carers are.

WHO ARE THE CARERS?

 ACTIVITY

❷

Write down all the people you can think of who care for others.

Here are a few suggestions to start you off:

- fathers/mothers
- friends
- social workers
- nurses.

How many people have you thought of? Did you remember to include yourself? Did you think of anyone whose job is not essentially caring but who often keeps a friendly eye on people, such as the milkman?

Your list of carers can probably be divided into three main groups:

- Those who are paid to care and who may have received some training, for example, nursing staff.
- Those who care voluntarily, perhaps through an organisation, for example, someone who helps out at a day centre or visits housebound elders.
- The family, who take a vast range of caring roles. This is the largest group of carers and the one which plays a major part in supporting the older community in the UK.

It is important to remember that the type of caring services available varies enormously from area to area. Services are dependent on many factors, e.g.

- local authority spending on caring services
- local demand for services
- community schemes and initiatives
- rural or town settings (affecting transport and distribution of resources).

If you think back to the settings where older people might be found, discussed earlier, you can now include the carers you will find working there. The following case studies look at some interesting situations.

CASE STUDY   *Living alone in the country*

Joan is 88 years old and lives alone in a small cottage in the Peak District. She can no longer walk to the shops, which are two miles away, because of arthritis. She is able to care for herself in her own home, although the household tasks would be too much to cope with if she had to do them all herself.

Joan receives the following support:

- Regular visits and phone calls from her son and daughter-in-law, who carry out house maintenance and look after the garden.

- A home carer visits twice-weekly, does the shopping and collects Joan's pension.
- The district nursing service provides help with bathing once a week.
- Meals on Wheels provide hot meals at lunch times.

CASE STUDY *Living in residential accommodation*

Balvinder is 86 years old and lives in a social services residential home. She came to the UK from Pakistan 20 years ago to join her son and daughter-in-law in London. Unfortunately she has outlived them both and has no other close relatives in this country. She speaks very little English and suffers from slight paralysis on her left side following a stroke.

She receives the following standard care:

- The care assistants at the home help her to wash, bath, dress, walk to the toilet and eat.
- A chiropodist visits the home and provides regular care to her feet.

The staff at the home had difficulty trying to help Balvinder overcome the effects

of bereavement and culture shock, which left her in a state of confusion and depression. The following measures were taken to lessen the trauma of culture shock:

- A care assistant who speaks Balvinder's language was assigned to do most of her care.

- Balvinder goes to a local day centre three days a week, which caters for Asian elders.
- The local Asian community has a rota to provide Indian cuisine.
- A local Asian family has adopted her as their grandmother and come to visit and take her out occasionally.

CASE STUDY *Living with a daughter or son and their family*

Richard is 91 years old. He lives with his daughter Emily and her husband Joe. Richard is diabetic and needs regular insulin injections. He suffers from arthritis and has impaired vision which means he needs help with all basic living tasks, e.g. bathing, washing, going to the toilet, dressing and feeding himself. He often gets up in the middle of

the night thinking that it is morning. Emily is responsible for most of his care.

Emily is exhausted. She has worked all her life and had often looked forward to retirement as a time when she could rest and do what she wanted to do. She feels that she has more work and ties now than she had even when the children

were small. Worse still, the stress of the situation is causing a lot of rows between herself and Joe.

The family receives the following support:

- A home carer comes in to help with the housework twice a week and she may do the shopping if Emily feels tired.
- The district nursing service provides help getting Richard up in the morning and putting him to bed at night. The district nursing sister gives him his injections of insulin for his diabetes and liaises with the family's doctor concerning his general health.
- Emily and Joe have been seeing a counsellor at Relate about their marital difficulties and she has suggested that they try to find further support in the home.

CASE STUDY *Living in sheltered accommodation*

Rosie and Edward have been married for over 60 years. They live together in a purpose-built bungalow within a small community designed especially for older people. This sheltered housing, as it is known, enables them to be fairly independent, and they have found this arrangement highly satisfactory.

There is a warden on the complex who keeps an eye on them and who can be available in minutes in an emergency. Laundry, recreational and dining facilities are available so that the elders can enjoy the company of other people of their own age and also be relieved of the burden of daily routine tasks.

ACTIVITY 3

1 Consider the responsibilities of the person who has to co-ordinate the sheltered care, and write down any you think of.

2 What sort of personal qualities do you think would be necessary to do this job well? For example, would it be important to be a well-organised person? Would it be important to understand older people's particular needs, fears and anxieties?

3 Imagine a day in the life of a warden and write a brief description.

4 If you know someone who cares for older people, arrange to interview them and compare what they say either with another carer or with your own experiences and ideas.

CASE STUDY   *Living in a long stay hospital*

Ethel has been a patient in the geriatric ward of a big Victorian hospital for twelve months. She broke her hip last winter when she was getting out of bed and lay helpless for 24 hours. When she was admitted to hospital she was extremely ill and was not expected to live very long.

Although her physical condition is now stable, she is frail, confused and incontinent. She requires full nursing care for all her basic living needs.

She receives the following care:

- Twenty-four-hour care from a team of nursing staff who are responsible for bathing, washing, prevention of pressure sores, dressing, feeding, managing Ethel's incontinence and for the implementation of a toilet training programme. They are also responsible for assessing Ethel's emotional state and considering the most appropriate caring response.
- Medical supervision from a team of doctors with a range of experience and training, including a consultant in charge who has specialist knowledge of caring for older people.
- Regular visits from a team of physio-

therapists who help Ethel with her mobility.
- Occupational therapy: a team of occupational therapists have implemented a programme of rehabilitation and recreation.

Ethel also receives visits from:

- A hospital social worker who supports Ethel's family and advises them about what to do regarding Ethel's home and future provision.
- Family members who bring Ethel fresh clothes, toiletries and personal treats.
- The hospital hairdresser.

Other hospital personnel employed in the care of Ethel include:

- Radiographers who took X-rays of her broken hip.
- Porters responsible for her transport from one part of the hospital to another.
- Dieticians who advise on the appropriate diet.
- Chefs who cook the meals.
- Pharmacists responsible for the provision of the drugs prescribed by the medical staff.
- Pathologists and biochemists who

determine types of infection and disease.

- Those providing a laundry service so that clean bed-linen, night clothes and towels are always available.
- A team of domestics to keep the wards clean, which is vital in the prevention of infectious disease.
- Administrators and clerical staff responsible for co-ordinating the smooth running of the hospital community, e.g. allocating the budget, filing and correspondence.
- People who maintain the building and equipment.

All of these personnel are involved in caring; some are much closer to Ethel and other patients than others, but their prime concern is the welfare of the sick.

CASE STUDY   *Living with foster carers*

Frances is an 82-year-old Afro-Caribbean woman who came to this country in 1955. She lived on her own as her family were in Jamaica and America. When Frances was 80 years old she entered residential accommodation because she was too frail to cope alone at home.

She was the only black person in the home and she became depressed and withdrawn following her admission. The social worker attached to the home suggested that she might be happier in a 'Home from Home' long-term placement with an Afro-Caribbean family. This was arranged and Frances is now settled with a foster family and her emotional condition has improved tremendously.

She receives the following support:

- Twenty-four-hour care from her foster family, which consists of help with dressing and bathing only.
- Regular visits from a chiropodist.
- A day centre she visits three times a week which caters for black elders and provides culturally appropriate food and entertainment.

- Regular visits and contact from the social worker, who continues to advise and support the family.

Note: Families are paid for fostering older adults in a similar way to those who foster children. You might like to find out if there is such a scheme in your area.

PERSONAL QUALITIES AND SKILLS OF CARERS

Having looked at who the carers in the community are, we can now consider the personal skills and qualities needed to be an effective carer. There is a wide range of caring jobs to suit people of varying abilities, skills and personality types (as you saw in the case studies above).

The skills required to care for others can be learnt. Consider the list of carers who have received either a formal training – for example, the social worker – or an informal one – for example, the warden or the home carer, whose suitability for the job may be relevant life experience.

Carers are human beings who need support like any other worker, even when they care for their own families. Knowing how to find support, where to go to and who to ask may be an important aspect. Imagination and resourcefulness may be useful qualities for carers.

  Make a list of qualities which you think are important in carers. As you read through the book or work with older people, you may wish to add to your list.

Here are some qualities you might put on your list:

- being a good listener
- assertiveness
- being a good organiser
- being able to put yourself in someone else's shoes
- resourcefulness
- imagination
- being hard working
- being fit and healthy
- flexiblility
- being willing to learn from others (including clients)
- reliability
- being punctual
- being sympathetic
- being able to manage stress.

LEARNING FROM OTHERS

If you feel someone is a good practitioner then you can adopt their strengths, and use them to improve your caring skills. If you feel someone is a poor practitioner, think about why. This can help you to avoid both the bad practice and perhaps also learn to avoid the route which caused it.

ATTITUDES AND CARERS

In Activity 4 you may have included feelings and attitudes in your list, on what caring means to you. Perhaps you have had the misfortune to receive an unsympathetic approach from a carer at some time in your life. It is an uncomfortable but valuable experience. There are several ways in which carers can make people feel distressed, not just by being unkind or by lacking in compassion.

If carers impose their religions or cultural beliefs on clients, or ridicule their client's values, it can be highly damaging to people's self-esteem. Equally, if a carer assumes a patronising attitude towards a client, perhaps because they consider that client to be incapable of making their own decisions, this again is damaging to a person's self-esteem and can create further dependence in the elder.

Earlier it was suggested that attitudes to ageing are influenced by role models, the media, cultural values and the society in which you live. It may be worthwhile examining your own attitudes to ageing, as well as those of the media, and see if you are surprised by what you discover.

ASSIGNMENT 1   OLDER PEOPLE AND THE MEDIA

1 Collect a supply of magazines and newspapers from family and friends. Use them to undertake the following tasks:

   (a) Count up all the pictures, including advertisements, and devise a simple table to show how many people in the illustrations fall into each of these categories:

   0–10 years   11–20 years   21–40 years   41–60 years   over 60 years

   (b) Choose one magazine and write a brief description of each picture in it, for example, 'young woman breastfeeding baby'.

   (c) Look at the pictures of younger people. What products are being advertised? What is the subject of the features in which they appear? What images of young people does this magazine conjure up for you?

   (d) Consider the pictures of older people. What products are being advertised? What sort of features do they appear in? What images of older people are being suggested?

   (e) Compare the images you have of younger and older people. Are there any differences? If so, have you tried to justify those differences to yourself? For example, if you found that there were no pictures at all of older people in a magazine about computers, would you say that was understandable because older people do not use or are not interested in computers?

2 Note down the television programmes which you would normally watch each week in order to monitor the images of people which they portray.

(a) Devise a simple table, giving title and type of programme, for example: Eastenders – soap opera.

Count the number of younger and older people featured in each programme.

(b) Choose one programme, or a series of advertisements and briefly describe what the younger people and the older people are doing.

(c) Describe the similarities and differences which you have found. What impressions are you left with?

When you have completed these exercises discuss your findings with a colleague. Were you surprised by your results?

If your feelings about ageing are negative (do you worry about grey hair?) try to think why this might be. Despite some wonderful role models in our society, like the three older adults at the beginning of the chapter, we are often bombarded with negative images of ageing and older people. This can result in ageist behaviour from some people who make disparaging assumptions about an older adult's abilities and discriminate accordingly.

If carers have a positive attitude to growing old and can continue to treat elders with dignity and respect when they are incontinent, frail and confused, they will have achieved a quality standard of caring.

Summary

This chapter asked you to think about what caring means to you, the variety of roles which carers have and what is meant by the term 'older people'.

There are two generations of older people over the age of 60 in our population. The very old often have no family to look after them and these people are increasing in the population. Ethnic elders are also increasing in numbers; their circumstances are considered further in the next chapter.

You also looked at the differing needs of older people living in rural surroundings, those in inner cities, those living with their families and those living in residential accommodation, and the wide range of caring roles which exist to meet those needs. The personal qualities and attitudes of carers and how these affect the ability to be a good practitioner were also considered.

❷ Families and Older People

Chapter 1 briefly considered the historical factors which explain the number of older adults in the population today. This chapter explores the role of the family in greater detail and looks at some older people's lives through case studies. As a carer it will help you to understand your clients better if you can appreciate the experiences which have influenced their lives. One way in which you can do this is through listening to older people reminiscing about the past.

FAMILY SUPPORT

Families can support their elders in the following ways:

- Providing love, affection, respect, security and a sense of belonging, which are vital to a person's emotional well-being, and promote and maintain self-esteem.
- Allowing them to provide help and support to younger, busier relatives, giving elders a sense of purpose and showing them that they are still useful and needed. The support may be either in the capacity of giving companionship or advice, or in practical ways such as caring for children, decorating or gardening.
- Acting as a support network to help elders retain or regain their independence following a temporary crisis, such as an illness, or a condition which has weakened or disabled them.
- Keeping an eye on an elder so that problems and difficulties can be avoided through early detection, for example, by changing a faulty light bulb on the stairs, or recommending a visit to the chiropodist.
- Providing visits and breaks that stimulate and enrich the lives of elders, who possibly could not afford such things on a pension, or who would find simply 'getting there' too much trouble.
- Providing a home for their older members when they become too frail to live on their own.
- Giving elders a sense of continuity. There is comfort in the knowledge that, as the end of your life approaches, your family are grown with children of their own and the pattern of life goes on.

FAMILY PATTERNS

Families are often put into two categories which help to identify the support network available. The categories, illustrated below, are the **nuclear family** and the **extended family**.

As you can see there are many more relatives in the extended family. If these relatives live in close contact with each other, either sharing the same household or

An extended family

neighbourhood, then they will be able to support each other and share family problems.

Sometimes families are split into nuclear units and live apart from each other – across a country or even in different parts of the world. This makes practical family support impossible, although financial help can be given. Contact is often maintained through writing letters, telephone calls and visits; some emotional support can be offered in this way, as well as help with decision making. However, it does not offset the problems of loneliness and isolation which many older people feel when separated from their families.

A nuclear family

One of the main forces that drives extended families apart is shortage of work. People sometimes move away from their local community to seek employment elsewhere, either in different parts of the country or abroad. Communities that depend on a large factory or mine for work can be broken by its closure. Wage earners move to areas of better employment in order to provide for themselves and their dependants.

Two world wars and the economic depression of the 1930s, together with the changing trends of employment, have contributed to the movement of people across the country away from their roots, sometimes to another country, e.g. emigration to Australia.

There are other reasons for emigrating and as these affect large numbers of elders living in Britain today, they will be looked at in the following pages.

OFFERING SUPPORT IN NUCLEAR FAMILIES

When families used to live in the same community and often in the same street, supporting older members was much easier. Routine care could be shared between several family members, who did not have to travel far in order to pop in and bring a meal or do the shopping.

Because so many people have now moved away from their local communities daily care for an elder often means bringing them into the family household. This may entail moving an older person from familiar surroundings, where they have lived all their life, to a strange district, which can leave them unable to go out without getting lost. The older adult loses contact with old friends and neighbours and can often become confused and disorientated.

The host family may have practical difficulties, for example, finding space, organising flexible working arrangements and coping with an increased workload. If the older adult becomes very frail or demented, their care can become a 24-hour job, which may isolate their primary carer from the outside world.

These difficulties can lead to increased tension within the family and strain relationships with partners, siblings and children. The health and well-being of carers is of paramount importance and the support of family carers is a crucial part of community care.

The care of the older old adult is usually undertaken by the younger old adult. You learnt in Chapter 1 (page 5) that many of the young old adults were from small families, so the care of their parents is more difficult to share. The younger old adult may not have the energy and strength to cope with a demanding care regime and may resent spending their retirement committed to such an arduous task. Often people are happy to take on the responsibility for older family members if they can be supported by resources and services in the community. These are examined further in Chapter 6.

As mentioned earlier there are a variety of reasons why people may have moved away from the extended family and these depend upon the historical and cultural background of the people as well as their individual circumstances.

It is important not to make assumptions about family patterns. For instance, it is often assumed that families are less caring about their older relatives because there are such large numbers of them who live on their own, but, as you have seen, that is in fact due to many of the older old people having no children.

ACTIVITY 1

Interview a family that cares for an older relative. Interview as many members of the family as possible and include the older adult as well. Try to find out as much as you can about the practical difficulties involved and what people feel about the situation.

This may be a sensitive issue; try to listen to what people are saying and do not press them to talk about anything which makes them feel uncomfortable.

If you belong to a student group, it may be useful to discuss the different family settings you have found with each other. You could consider solutions to any problems which families may have encountered.

Carers often think that people from the ethnic minority communities care for their elders better and assume family support exists when, in fact, this may not be the case. The migration of nuclear family units can leave some ethnic elders without support from both their families and the community provision.

The following section explores some of the historical reasons for migration of ethnic minority people to the UK.

MIGRATION TO BRITAIN

Throughout history the population of Britain has changed due to immigration and emigration. The large numbers of people who emigrated to the Commonwealth countries after the First World War have already been mentioned. There have been black people in the UK for many centuries – their presence was recorded in Elizabethan times.

A major reason for emigration – leaving one's own country – is to escape tyranny and oppression. Hundreds of thousands of Jews and political refugees came to the UK in the 1930s for this reason. Many Polish and Ukrainian people came during the Second World War when their countries were invaded.

There was great unrest in 1947 after India was partitioned and there were people from the Indian sub-continent who decided to seek a better life for themselves in the UK.

In the 1950s the UK suffered a great labour shortage, particularly in the industries which depended heavily on manpower. People from the West Indies and other New Commonwealth countries were encouraged to come to the UK to take up this work. At that time the islands of the West Indies were gaining their independence, unemployment was high, and so the mass migration of people from the West Indies to the UK began. Initially skilled middle class workers migrated from the Caribbean, creating further difficulties for the communities left behind.

Of the people who came here in the 1950s from the Caribbean 90 per cent were under 50 years old. These people, together with the Asians, Jews and Polish people who emigrated here in the middle of the century, form a large minority of our older population today.

Migration has many shocks for immigrants trying to integrate into a new society. Some of these do not become fully apparent until old age. The following case studies will give you some idea of the experiences of elders who migrated.

CASE STUDY   *The Afro-Caribbean experience*

Mr Thompson, aged 67, a retired bus driver.

'I came over to this country in 1958. There was plenty of work then and I got a job straight away. It was a start and my wife came over to join me soon afterwards. The two eldest children stayed with their grandmother in Jamaica but the two youngest came to live with us.

We never expected to stay so long – but the years pass by and we've put down our roots here. The children went to school and we bought a house. My wife was working, and we thought that we were giving our daughters a good start by educating them here.

Many of us expected our children to do well and get good jobs – but unemployment is high in this area, particularly for black people.

We've thought about going back to Jamaica but our friends have either moved or died – there's no one left that we know now. Our eldest children are grown up and live in Canada and the USA.

The two youngest are married with children of their own but they've moved to London – we see them occasionally. We didn't really earn enough money to save for our retirement and we always thought that we would return home. Elders are respected in Jamaica, not like in Britain.

I don't feel that this country is our home; black people still aren't accepted here. I worry about what will happen when one of us goes. I do feel bitter sometimes to think that we worked so hard and sacrificed so much to end our days like this.'

CASE STUDY   *The Polish and Eastern European experience*

Mrs Alekna, aged 72, is a housewife who was widowed two years ago.

'I came to this country in 1945 and I can never return to my homeland of Poland. I left behind my parents and brothers and sisters and I haven't seen them since that

time. I brood about this often, it makes me very depressed, particularly now I'm on my own. It was very hard for me when I lost my husband. I have a son who lives locally and he pops in to see me every week with his family, but they have their own lives to lead.

I know some other Polish people in the local community; several of us settled in this town. They feel the same way as I do.

When you are younger and looking after a family or working you can cope.

Sometimes when the older ones go senile they can only speak Polish, they forget their English altogether. This worries me greatly, particularly as my son can't speak any Polish at all. How could we talk to each other? I miss my family more now than I ever have before.'

CASE STUDY   *The South Asian experience*

Mrs Patel is a housewife aged 60.

'We came here in 1953. There had been trouble at home and we knew a friend who had settled in Britain. He said it was a good place, but we started off in a bedsitter. I had two children of two and three years old. I remember being very

depressed when I first came. My husband was out at work all day. I was lonely and couldn't speak any English. I missed my mother and sisters very much. Many women suffer like this still today when they come here.

We've worked hard and bought this house. My eldest son and his wife live here, and their two children. My other son lives in the next street with his family. They often come round here so we can all eat together.

My husband retires next year. I'm glad my children are near me. We often speak to my sister on the phone – she still lives in India. They ask our advice on family matters which is nice – we are very close.

We are Hindus and my husband and I are in the third stage of our lives, called the Vanaprastha. This is the stage when you have grandchildren and you become more concerned with religious matters. My religion is a great comfort to me and I have looked forward to this stage of my life.

I tried to get my mother to come and live with me but she wasn't allowed to come in because of immigration rules. I miss her and I worry about her a lot. It has been hard here but I don't complain. I know I'm luckier than some.'

Older adults from the ethnic minority communities face all the problems that old age brings, but these are compounded by added difficulties, for example:

- Loss of family support. The family may have been split by migration and immigration laws which prevent family members from joining relatives in Britain.
- Poverty. Many immigrants accepted low income jobs and have not managed to save a nest egg for their retirement. Some send money home to support their families, draining their own resources.
- Racism. Racism may affect all aspects of life, including health care, housing, and employment, and elders may fear for their personal safety.
- Language and communication difficulties. Elders may speak little or no English, either because they have not been able to learn it or because they have reverted back to their heritage language through loneliness or short-term memory loss. Some immigrated to the UK as older adults to join their grown-up children here and have found it difficult to learn English. A research project undertaken in Birmingham by AFFOR in 1981, called 'Elders of the Minority Ethnic Groups', showed that 88 per cent of Asian elders questioned in the survey did not speak English.
- Communication with community workers and even family members may be difficult and claiming benefits to which older people are entitled may be a problem if they cannot read or write English.
- Loneliness and isolation. Elders who have no family in this country may feel like 'foreigners' in a hostile community and may become seriously depressed.

ACTIVITY

1 Imagine you are a widower, aged 70, who lives alone. Describe a day in your life. Include things like what time you get up, what you do all day, what you eat, and your thoughts and feelings.

2 Every weekend your daughter visits you. Write about what you do together, whether you look forward to these visits and if so why?

3 Interview an older adult about a typical day in their life. Try to talk to someone who lives alone (this is not essential) and compare their day with the one you imagined.

SUPPORT FROM OUTSIDE THE FAMILY

The cornflake family is an expression that is used to describe the ideal family as represented by the advertisements on television. These families are always well dressed, clean and happy. The sun is always shining and their house is tidy and expensively furnished. They do not seem to have real problems like we do, the people watching at home.

If you did Assignment 1 (page 18) you may have come across the 'cornflake granny' on the television advertisements.

She was probably sweet and kind with grey or white hair, perhaps with young grandchildren. We considered the effect the media has on our thinking in Chapter 1 through the assignment at the end. It is important to remember that older adults have a variety of family circumstances just like anyone else.

There are people living in Britain today from many different cultures who are supported by a strong and caring extended family but there are also individuals from those cultures who do not have that support. People can end up alone through childlessness, death, divorce, family breakdown, imprisonment or migration. Occasionally elders who belong to an extended family can be neglected and forgotten. Traditionally, married or single women looked after dependent elders but today many more women are working to support their families and may find the care of older relatives an impossible commitment.

SUPPORT FROM FRIENDS

Often people who are separated from their families turn to friends for love, support and companionship. These relationships can sustain people in their younger years when they are leading busy lives. Unfortunately older people can lose touch with their friends through death, illness or disability and lack of mobility. For example, two elderly widows may be great friends, meeting daily for a chat and a coffee. If one of these elders has a stroke and is admitted to hospital the other may find herself unable to cope with this loss and become withdrawn, depressed and increasingly housebound.

Making new friends later in life can be very hard; often older people feel they 'cannot be bothered' to make the effort, particularly if they are grieving the loss of a partner or a close friend. It is also less easy to meet new people unless they belong to a local club or visit a day centre. This is difficult if people are disabled and find travelling awkward, if not impossible. Some centres have their own transport, but they also have waiting lists and there is insufficient provision for all who want or need it.

SUPPORT FROM VARIOUS ORGANISATIONS

Religious organisations play a major part in supporting elders and provide great social as well as spiritual comfort. A research project, 'Race, Health and Welfare' by Dr C.S. Fenton, undertaken in Bristol in 1983–84, suggests that ethnic older adults in general do not attend or belong to community groups or associations except of a religious kind. The research also suggests that the church associations of Afro-Caribbean elders in particular offer tremendous social support.

Often local community initiatives set up visiting schemes where volunteers visit housebound or lonely older adults in their homes. Voluntary organisations like Age Concern or local religious bodies may provide luncheon clubs, day centres and self-help groups.

Social services will sometimes pay people a small wage to visit an older adult regularly to see that they are alright, and perhaps do a bit of shopping or bring a meal round and stay for a chat.

Social workers and local voluntary organisations are likely to be aware of any local schemes which can provide companionship, and these are worth contacting if any older adult or their carer would like to know what is available. There may be local facilities, particularly in inner city areas, which provide for the cultural needs of ethnic elders. Social services, community leaders and advice centres may be aware of any such local schemes.

Other support systems available to help people who have no family will be discussed in detail in Chapter 6. These include the statutory voluntary and private caring services which exist to support the carers so that elders can continue to be looked after by their families.

LIFE HISTORIES OF OLDER PEOPLE

If you are going to care for older people in their homes or in residential accommodation, either supporting or substituting their families, then you should be aware of the many changes which have affected their lives. This will help you as a carer for the following reasons:

- As people age their long-term memory remains intact and it is often the recent past which may be forgotten or become unfamiliar, so an understanding of an elder's distant past is relevant and useful to carers.
- You will be able to appreciate the values and attitudes of older people. For example, in the early twentieth century inflation was virtually unheard of and prices remained constant for years. Many people were poor and patched and mended their possessions. There was no social security or free health service and people depended on their family and neighbours, or parish handouts, when times were hard. Older people who remember this often find the 'throw-away' affluence of today's society alien and frightening.
- You may increase your respect for older adults when you consider the enormous challenges that they have met and overcome. For example, the very old adult will have lived through several wars, and may have lost family members and friends in them.
- You will remember that the frail person before you, who needs your care, was once an active and independent person who deserves to be treated with dignity.

   To study a banyan tree, you not only must know its main stem in its soil, but also must trace the growth of its greatness in the further soil, for then you can know the true nature of its vitality.

   Tagore Radindranath quoted in Tinker, H. (1977), *The Banyan Tree*

The following case study looks at the life of a woman born at the turn of the century and traces some of the social, economic and industrial changes that have taken place during her lifetime.

CASE STUDY   *The life of Mary Lewis*

Mary Lewis was born at home in Netherton near Dudley in the Black Country, in 1901. Her father was a chainmaker and had a workshop in the main yard which was shared by the surrounding terrace houses. He earned £1 a week which was good money – far more than the nailmakers were paid. Mary's mother made small chains in the workshop, but she also spent many hours looking after the fire in the house, washing and cooking.

Beer was a popular drink in the Black Country; the public houses provided a haven from overcrowded homes and harsh working conditions, and many people brewed their own ale at home in the wash-house. Family life focused on the kitchen and all the cooking was done on the range over the open fire. The house was lit by gas lamps or candles at night.

Although times were hard Mary was lucky; her family could afford to buy shoes for the children and to send them to school. School was very cold in the winter as there was no heating and it often closed when too many of the children were off sick with common illnesses such as diphtheria, measles, chicken pox and scarlet fever. Dudley was a very unhealthy place to live – only three out of ten people lived to be 20 years old. The family shared a toilet (a wooden box which was emptied once a month) with several other families. This, plus the large amount of horses in the streets and pigs kept in yards, meant that flies were a major health hazard. Mary had five brothers and sisters but three of them died from illnesses before they were five years old. The doctor's services were expensive and even the

chainmaker's family could not always afford to send for him.

All the families around the main yard had shares in a pig which they divided up amongst them when it was killed: everything was used except the 'squale' (squeal)!

In 1914 war was declared against Germany. Mary's two elder brothers went to fight in the war and both were killed. In all 744 000 men were killed, devastating many families, including Mary's.

Mary continued to live with her mother and father through the jazz era of the 1920s. She witnessed the creation of the first unions, culminating in the General Strike of 1926; the depression of the 1930s, the Second World War and the rationing of food and clothes which lasted till 1954. She lived through the evolution of the Welfare State and the establishment of a free Health Service, and she witnessed living standards rise and the demise of the pawn shop.

Mary's father died in 1945 and her brothers and sisters moved away. The end of the war saw an industrial boom and the creation of employment opportunities all over the country caused the dispersal of many families. In 1961 Mary started drawing her old age pension. She had never married and was caring for her mother in a maisonette in Dudley. Their family home, along with many other houses in the area, had been knocked down and cleared for new development.

Today Mary lives alone in Dudley. She has lost contact with most of her nieces and nephews and none of them live in the Black Country now. She has a nephew who comes to see her sometimes when he passes through Dudley on business.

Although Mary still knows many people in the area a lot of her friends have died or gone into residential accommodation. She is often lonely and thinks wistfully of the days when houses were full of people popping in and out all day long.

It is sometimes said of old people that they do not like change but they have seen more changes in their lifetime than any other generation before them. Today we have a very different world.

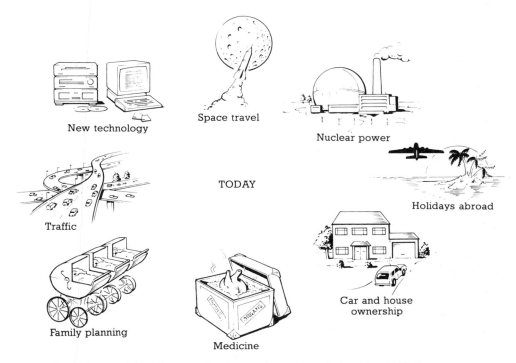

New technology

Space travel

Nuclear power

TODAY

Traffic

Holidays abroad

Family planning

Medicine

Car and house ownership

Figure 2.1   *Some of the changes that have taken place during Mary's lifetime*

ASSIGNMENT 2   **A LIFE HISTORY**

Interview an older person about their life history. Ask them questions about what they did when they were a child, what school was like and how much food and clothes cost.

If you interview someone who has lived locally all their lives it will be interesting to find out how the locality has changed. If you interview someone who immigrated here ask them what they can remember of their home country. You may find it useful to have some old photographs from the local library or suggest using some of the elder's own photographs to help jog their memory.

THE LIBRARY
GUILDFORD COLLEGE
of Further and Higher Education

Sometimes it helps to interview a married couple or two friends together as they can remind each other of events that happened years ago. You may like to use a tape recorder if your interviewees are willing, as this would be useful to play to others in your group.

Summary

This chapter looked at how families can support older people in many different ways, including practically, financially and emotionally. However, not everyone belongs to a supportive family, perhaps because of family break-down, childlessness, migration or death. Older people with no family to support them may rely on friends, their religion and voluntary organisations. Friends, in particular, can be a great comfort to each other but they too may be separated by illness, death or disability.

Migration is one of the primary reasons why some older people have no family support today. Many people who immigrated here in the 1930s, 1940s and 1950s will be elders now. Ethnic elders may suffer problems in addition to those experienced by indigenous elders, including racism, poverty and communication difficulties.

Finally, it is important that you are aware of and appreciate the life history of elders, as it will help you to empathise with those in your care.

③ *The Ageing Process*

Chapter 2 looked at the role of the family in the care and support of older people, and examined the lives and experiences of some older people. This chapter concentrates on the way in which people age and how external factors can affect the ageing process.

THE CYCLE OF LIFE

During our lives we grow and develop physically, emotionally, intellectually, socially and spiritually. We interact with our environment and, if conditions are favourable, we are able to move forward to realise our potential, whatever that may be.

Abraham Maslow (1962) proposed a theory about human needs. He suggested that there is a hierarchy of basic needs (see Figure 3.1) and that each level of need has to be met before a person can move on to the next stage. For example, the physiological needs, such as food, oxygen, water, sleep and elimination (passing urine and faeces) must be met before a person can concern themselves with safety and security.

Figure 3.1   *Maslow's Hierarchy of Needs*

When these needs have been satisfied, love and belonging can be addressed, which leads an individual on to self-esteem. Only when all of these have been satisfied can someone move onto self-actualisation, i.e. fulfilling self-potential.

The process of life involves growing up to become an independent adult who invests in the next generation, perhaps by bringing up a family or by serving the community through paid or voluntary employment. This process is a cycle whereby the adult slows down after the productive years and finally, when the body systems are worn out, the adult dies.

Newer, younger generations continue the cycle, nurturing their offspring and growing old in their turn. We are familiar with this pattern of birth, death and rebirth, which we witness through seasonal changes in our environment each year, as leaves are lost in autumn and new growth appears in spring.

It is important to emphasise this point so that the distinction can be made between ageing which is inevitable, and ill-health which is not. For example, Alzheimer's disease, Parkinson's disease, stroke and diabetes are diseases which commonly affect older people, but they are not part of the ageing process itself.

There are different perspectives on ageing which consider how individuals develop as they grow older; this chapter looks briefly at the biological, sociological and psychological theories of the ageing process. It is particularly concerned with how biological ageing affects people and how good health may be maintained through this process.

PSYCHOLOGICAL THEORIES OF AGEING

Psychological theories about ageing are concerned with an older adult's behaviour, personal development, feelings and reactions to situations.

Sullivan (1953) and Erikson (1963) both consider a developmental approach to ageing which theorises that the personality needs to go through a series of stages, from infancy through to adulthood and finally senescence (from 65–100 years of age). It is necessary for people to develop successfully through each of these various stages in order to cope with the demands of later life.

Sullivan believes maturity is reached if someone can form satisfactory personal relationships amongst family and friends. Erikson believes that the stage of adulthood (from 25–65 years) needs to be creative and productive and that in order to pass through this stage satisfactorily people need to have been involved with the next generation. This can be achieved without having children through an individual's work or leisure activities.

Senescence, the final stage of Erikson's developmental journey is labelled 'Integrity *vs* Despair'. Erikson believes that if someone can look back on their life feeling satisfied with their accomplishments they have a sense of integrity. If, however, they feel their life has had no meaning and has been a waste of time they feel a sense of despair.

SOCIOLOGICAL THEORIES OF AGEING

Sociological theories on ageing are concerned with the older individual's relationship with society and the cultural, class, socio-economic and family influences which affect longevity and behaviour in old age.

THE LIBRARY
GUILDFORD COLLEGE
of Further and Higher Education

DISENGAGEMENT THEORY

The disengagement theory was suggested by Cummings and Henry in 1961. The theory states that older people and society disengage from each other as a process which is a preparation for death. For example, when someone retires at 65 they disengage from the business world and telephone friends less, losing contact and, in this way, became free to enjoy old age.

ACTIVITY THEORY

The activity theory (Havighurst, 1963) suggests that older people should remain 'engaged' with society and be active members of society, taking on new roles and responsibilities, e.g. doing voluntary work, becoming more involved in religious affairs or learning a new skill.

CONTINUITY THEORY

The continuity theory (Neugarten, 1964) is concerned with personality. It suggests that as people age they become more predictable in their behaviour, alter their sex-role perception, are less anxious about peer group pressure and become more introspective. This change is called interiority and is part of an individual's preoccupation with reviewing their life and its worth.

HOW CAN THIS HELP CARERS?

If carers are aware of these different theories on ageing it can help their understanding of the life cycle as a continuing process and offer further insight into the behaviour of older people. Carers should consider the biological, cultural, sociological and psychological influences on ageing and how these affect individuals in their care.

In practical terms this may be done best by discussing care problems with other carers and formulating constructive care plans which take into account an individual's personality and needs. A good example of this was illustrated in the case study of Balvinder Sander in Chapter 1, where the cultural needs of a client were considered in the formation of a care plan. Care plans need to be frequently reviewed and assessed so that they can be responsive to an older adult's ageing process.

BIOLOGICAL AGEING

Biologically people age in different ways; some individuals age more quickly than others and not all parts of the body age at the same rate. Ageing is a natural process which is brought about by changes in cells and this usually begins when people are in their twenties.

A good example of this is grey hair. Grey hair is hair without any pigment, caused by cellular changes in the **hair follicle**. It is more common in older people but affects younger people in varying degrees. Less visible cell changes are taking place throughout our lives and, like greying hair, they affect some people more than others. Ageing is the accumulation of many cell changes over a long period of time.

THE EFFECTS OF CELL CHANGES ON THE BODY SYSTEMS

Our bodies are made up of billions of tiny units called cells. Each cell is programmed by information contained in the chemical DNA (deoxyribonucleic acid) to perform a specific function and to replace itself when it is damaged or worn out. All cells need oxygen and nutrients to live and function and in doing so they create waste products. This process is called **metabolism**. The transport system which provides the cells with oxygen and nutrients and which removes the waste products is called the **circulatory system**.

The cells are programmed to make up our various tissues and organs which together form our body systems. These organs and systems are interdependent and the body has several mechanisms for ensuring a balanced internal environment. This is called **homeostasis**.

There are several theories on the ageing process which try to explain why cells deteriorate or die and the loss of function which ensues, as illustrated in Figure 3.2.

So what is the effect of cell change, cell death and an inability to replace every cell that is worn out? The overall effect is a decline in function and efficiency of body systems, a slower metabolism and diminishing strength. The ageing body strives for homeostasis and is usually successful in a stable, familiar environment, but it cannot cope easily with stress, change or illness.

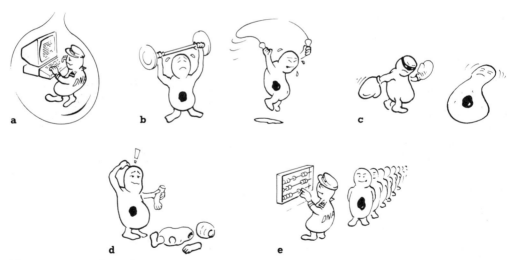

Figure 3.2   **a   Genetic**
Is life span programmed into the genes before birth?
b   Wear and tear
As cells wear out, are we less able to replace them?
c   Immune system
As older cells change are they attacked by the body's own immune system?
d   Error
As cells age do they make more mistakes in trying to replace themselves?
e   Cell death
Are the number of times the cell can reproduce itself programmed into the cell?

As body systems are interdependent, the effects of ageing can be cumulative, with the inefficiency of one system impairing the function of another (see Figure 3.3). For example, if the circulatory system is impaired it affects the transport of oxygen and nutrients to all the cells in the body, which in turn threatens the ability of the cells to function properly.

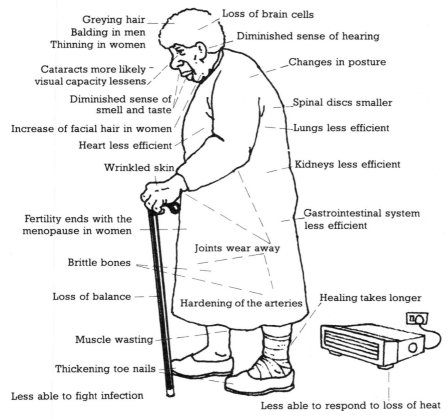

Figure 3.3   *Biological ageing*

THE CIRCULATORY SYSTEM

The circulatory system is made up of the heart and the blood vessels. The vessels taking blood from the heart are called **arteries**. The tiny ones which take blood to the cells are called **capillaries** and those which return blood to the heart are called **veins**.

As the heart ages so its muscle fibres diminish and are replaced by fatty and connective tissue fibres. The valves inside the heart harden and so the pumping action becomes less efficient. This affects the cardiac output, i.e. the volume of blood which is pumped out of the heart.

As the arteries age they also become harder and less elastic, a condition known as **arteriosclerosis**. This means that the arteries cannot carry the same volume of blood that they once could. These hardened arteries are often further impaired by **atherosclerosis,** a condition in which fatty deposits are laid down on the lining of the arteries. This makes the insides of the vessels narrower, not only further diminishing the blood volume but also increasing the blood pressure within them.

Atherosclerosis increases the risk of clot formation in these narrow passages, which in turn can result in heart attacks and strokes. It is a diseased state which is very common in the Western world and begins to form in people at an early age. It is not an inevitable part of human ageing as the incidence of this disease in some other parts of the world is very low. It is thought that smoking, obesity, a diet high in animal fats and low in fibre, lack of exercise, stress and alcohol consumption may be contributory factors in the development of this disease.

Blood is returned to the heart through large veins situated between muscle groups which are able to pump the blood upwards. Valves in the veins prevent back flow. Inactivity of an elder can reduce this return of the blood to the heart and, as the valves age, they become less efficient, resulting in varicose veins in the legs. These are more common in women, possibly because pregnancy is also a contributory factor.

THE RESPIRATORY SYSTEM

The respiratory system is closely connected to the circulatory system. The right side of the heart pumps blood through to the lungs so the carbon dioxide in red blood cells can be exchanged for oxygen which is present in the air sacs of the lungs. The red blood cells take on board the oxygen and give up their carbon dioxide by a process of exchange called **diffusion**.

As people age the sacs in the lungs responsible for gas exchange tend to burst and form larger sacs which reduces the flexibility of the lungs and therefore the amount of oxygen that can be obtained from each breath.

THE BRAIN AND THE NERVOUS SYSTEM

The brain consists mainly of ten to twelve billion cells called **neurones**, which are responsible for the co-ordination of body systems and for interaction with the external environment. They also play a part in determining intelligence and personality.

From the age of 25 we lose 10 000 brain cells per day and the speed at which messages are transmitted along our nervous system may decrease by about 10 per cent with age. Brain cells are the only cells which do not replace themselves. The nerve pathways which form our memory would be lost if all brain cells were replaced in the recycling process which happens to other cells. Imagine the chaos of having to learn how to walk, talk, feed yourself and use the toilet every seven years or so!

Some functions of the brain are less efficient in an older adult, e.g. short-term memory recall is more difficult than long-term memory recall. However the intelligence of an individual is not thought to be affected by this loss of brain cells. Although an older person's ability to learn new skills may be slower, this may be balanced by other factors, such as motivation and previous knowledge.

Diminished intellectual ability in old age is not part of the ageing process, but may be the result of diseases such as Alzheimer's disease, or atherosclerosis of the arteries which supply blood to the brain. It may also be caused by depression or social isolation and loss of conversational skills.

THE SENSES

Sight

The lens in the eye is responsible for focusing and it does this by changing shape. An ageing lens is less able to do this and so older people may become long-sighted. This can be easily corrected by wearing glasses for activities such as reading and sewing.

Hearing

Some hearing loss is experienced by many older people. This may be caused by changes in the inner ear where sound transmissions are sent to the brain via the auditory nerve. Changes in the inner ear may also affect an elder's balance and this increases the incidence of falls.

People who have been exposed to noisier environments in their lives will be more susceptible to hearing loss. Unfortunately not all hearing impairment can be helped by a hearing aid.

Smell and taste

Our sense of taste is a combination of messages sent to the brain from our taste buds in the tongue and from sensory receptors responsible for picking up smells in our noses. Both senses diminish with age with the actual loss of taste buds. If food tastes blander and different foods taste similar, this may contribute to a loss of appetite.

THE MUSCULO-SKELETAL SYSTEM

The musculo-skeletal system is made up of bones, joints and muscles. It gives our bodies shape, protects our vital organs and major blood vessels and, working in conjunction with the nervous system, provides us with our mobility.

As the body ages changes take place in the bone mass, joints and muscles, sometimes adversely affecting mobility which in turn can have a major effect on the life of an elder. Ageing bone tissue may lose mass and become more porous and brittle. This condition is called **osteoporosis** and is particularly common in post-menopausal women (see page 41). The loss of **oestrogen** is thought to be responsible for the failure to maintain a correct balance of calcium between the body and bone tissue, resulting in a decrease in bone mass.

A diet deficient in vitamin D and calcium combined with a sedentary lifestyle can worsen the condition, although vegetarians appear to have some protection. **Hormone replacement therapy** can be given after the menopause to help prevent its occurrence, but this treatment is not always offered by GPs. If an elder with this disease should fall the brittle bones are much more likely to fracture.

Cartilage, which lies between the discs of the spine and forms the ends of joints, calcifies and hardens. This, combined with the changes to the spinal vertebrae that occur with ageing, results in changes in height and posture and curving of the spine. Joints may become stiff and painful, restricting movement. **Osteoarthritis** is a condition where the joints have been affected in this way. The weight-bearing joints, e.g. the hip, are more commonly affected. The condition appears to be more common in women than men, and obesity is a contributory factor.

Muscles waste as we grow older and in the process some muscle cells are replaced by fatty tissue. The muscles subsequently become less powerful. This may affect respiration, digestion and bladder control as well as mobility and strength.

NAILS AND FEET

Nails thicken with age and become more difficult to cut, particularly toenails. The feet need special care in old age for several reasons:

- elders are more likely to suffer from chilblains
- sores and cuts will take longer to heal as the circulation to the foot is furthest from the heart
- damaged and painful feet will badly affect an older adult's mobility and possibly their independence.

People who suffer from diabetes or circulatory problems are at special risk from poor healing and should have their feet attended to by a chiropodist.

TEETH

In the Western world 75 per cent of people aged 75 and over have lost their teeth. Evidence suggests that our diet, high in sugar and low in fibre, is a major cause of this.

Well-fitting dentures are essential for people to maintain a good dietary intake and also to preserve speech, social contact and self-esteem. Regular check-ups are important as gums recede and the dentures may loosen and not fit properly after a while.

SKIN

The skin forms a protective layer preventing loss of moisture from within and penetration of micro-organisms from outside. It has a major role in temperature regulation and it contains many sensory neurones which carry messages to the brain and inform us about our immediate environment. There is a layer of fat beneath our skin and the skin contains elastic fibres which enable it to stretch and return. As we age the skin loses the elasticity and is less able to 'spring back' into place. The layer of fat may be less, so that the skin hangs loosely and there may also be pigment changes and less sebaceous and sweat glands. This changes the appearance of the skin, resulting in wrinkles, particularly on the face, neck and the looser skin on the body. Exposure to the sun, smoking and a poor diet increase the ageing process of the skin.

The sensory receptors in the skin become less sensitive to drops in temperature – elders may be found sitting in a chilly room insisting that they 'don't feel cold', putting themselves at risk of **hypothermia** by allowing their body temperature to fall.

HAIR

Hair growth slows down and there are changes in pigment cells which result in grey hair. Hair loss increases with age, particularly in men. Women may also lose their hair, particularly at the temples and on the top of the head. Women may grow more facial hair after the menopause when they no longer produce oestrogen.

THE DIGESTIVE SYSTEM

There are so many age-related factors affecting dietary intake – including social, emotional, financial and practical factors – that it is difficult to know which is cause and which is effect. You have seen that the loss of teeth and sense of taste and smell are part of the ageing process. Older people also produce less saliva which may make food difficult to swallow. **Peristalsis**, which is the wave-like motion that passes food along the gastro-intestinal tract, slows down. Muscle wasting affects this body system as much as any other, so that the muscles in the stomach and intestines are weaker. The effect is an increased tendency to suffer from heartburn and constipation.

THE URINARY SYSTEM

The kidneys contain one million **nephrons** each. The nephron is responsible for filtering urea from the blood, and for the reabsorption of nutrients and useful substances into the blood. Nephrons are lost from the kidneys as we grow older, so that by the age of 75 only 65 per cent of the original amount remain and, by the age of 90, only 53 per cent.

As we age changes also take place in the bladder and lower urinary tract which are discussed in detail in Chapter 4. An understanding of these changes is essential for the prevention, treatment and rehabilitation of incontinence.

THE REPRODUCTIVE TRACT

Women lose the ability to have children after the **menopause**. The menopause normally occurs between the ages of 40 and 55. The ovaries stop producing eggs each month and menstruation ceases. This affects the amount of oestrogen and **progesterone** (the female hormones) normally produced by the ovarian follicles.

Hormone replacement therapy may be given to women if they experience distressing symptoms at this time, for example, hot flushes or night sweats, or it may be given to prevent osteoporosis (see page 39).

As a woman ages the vagina may become dry and smaller and the walls may become thinner. It is possible for older women to enjoy fulfilling sexual relationships despite these changes, possibly with the aid of a lubricating gel if dryness is a problem. It is more likely to be the unavailability of a partner or society's taboos on sexual activity of elders which inhibit an enjoyable sex life rather than any reason due to biological ageing.

Men continue to produce sperm and **testosterone** throughout their lives. The quality of the sperm becomes less fertile but they are still able to father a child well into old age. Sexual potency diminishes with age so that a man takes longer both to get an erection and to ejaculate. Although impotency is more common amongst older men it is not an inevitable part of ageing. Men with this condition should seek appropriate treatment for it, just as they would have done if they had been younger.

You can see how the ageing process is part of a life cycle and that it is influenced by our individual personalities and experiences. A creative and productive life which has provided personal fulfilment will give a sense of meaning and integrity to an older person. Alternatively a sense of loss and sometimes despair is felt by older people who have not managed to achieve their hopes or dreams or who have been disappointed with their life's achievements.

Despite the many bodily changes that take place in the process of ageing, older adults often cope well in familiar surroundings. However, the ageing body copes less well with illness, is less able to fight infection, takes longer to heal wounds and the stress of surgery is far more traumatic. Emotional stress also takes its toll on older people. This is explored further in Chapter 5.

ACTIVITY

1 What is the difference between atherosclerosis and arteriosclerosis?

2 Why are women particularly prone to
   (a) osteoporosis
   (b) varicose veins?

3 Name two diseases which are commonly found amongst older people but which are not part of the ageing process.

4 Name three factors which increase the effects of ageing on the skin.

5 What is meant by the term homeostasis?

6 By the age of 90 what percentage of nephrons are remaining in the kidney?

7 Short-term memory recall diminishes with age. What advantages do older adults have over younger people to enable them to counteract this, when learning new skills?

8 Two fit and healthy women, one a young woman of 20, the other an elder of 70, run a 100-metre race. What biological advantages does the younger woman have over her rival?

FACTORS AFFECTING LENGTH OF LIFE

The first part of this chapter established that people age in different ways and at different rates and explored a few basic theories on how and why this ageing occurs. This section considers the effect of *environmental* factors on ageing.

When the example of the condition atherosclerosis was given earlier in the chapter it was suggested that the main causes of this disease were people's behaviour and lifestyle. Ageing is a process which involves and is influenced by genetic, psychological, socio-economic, cultural and environmental factors. For example, as the skin ages it wrinkles due to loss of moisture and elastic fibres. The rate of all change is influenced by the genetic material in the skin cells inherited from our parents, and the treatment of the skin by ourselves and our climate. The application of creams and lotions will be influenced by our gender and cultural background.

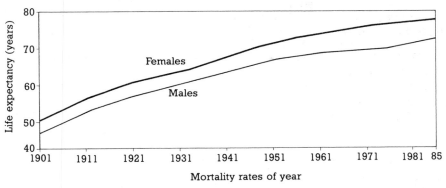

Figure 3.4   *Expectation of life at birth, by sex this century*

Source: *Social Trends 19*, © Crown copyright 1989. Reproduced courtesy of HMSO

LIFE EXPECTANCY

In this century the average life expectancy has risen considerably, due to the social and medical improvements which we discussed earlier (see Figure 3.4).

Figure 3.5 shows that the life expectancy rates for women are consistently higher than those for men. This is found to be the case in other cultures and races studied. It appears that females have a genetic advantage over males regarding longevity (length of life) if the statistics are taken from the same socio-economic group.

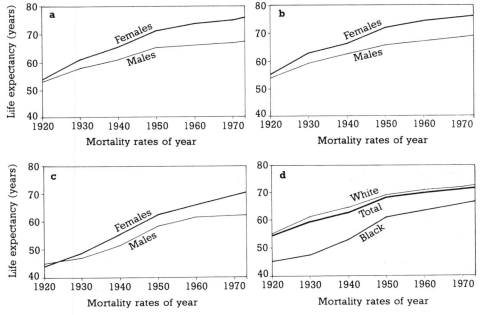

Figure 3.5   **a**   *Expectation of life at birth, total population of US*
             b   *Expectation of life at birth, white population of US*
             c   *Expectation of life at birth, black population of US*
             d   *Expectation of life at birth, white, black and total populations of US*

The socio-economic factor is considered in several of the following examples. For statistical purposes our society is divided into different groups in order to compare a variety of data, for example on lifestyles, health, education and housing. These groups are based on both social and economic factors and are compiled according to people's employment and wealth.

If you look at Figure 3.5, which shows the expectation of life at birth in the United States from 1920–73, you can see a comparison between the white and black population. White women and black women live longer than the men in their racial group. However, life expectancy rates for white males and black females are much closer. In certain years (particularly in the earlier part of the century) white males have

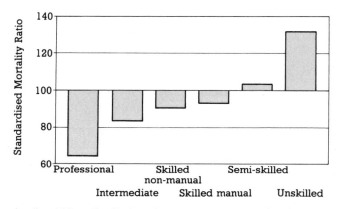

Figure 3.6 *Standardised Mortality Ratios of men aged 16–64 by social class, 1981–83*

Source: *Social Trends 19,* © Crown copyright 1989. Reproduced courtesy of HMSO

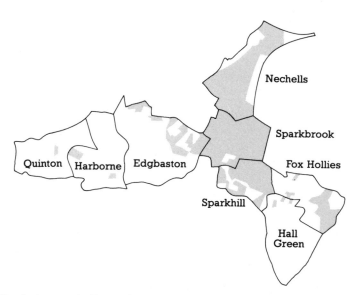

Figure 3.7 *Shaded areas indicate the most deprived areas within the Central Birmingham Health Authority*

experienced greater life expectancy than black females. The differences in life expectancy between black and white people may be due to the poverty and poorer living conditions of the black population.

These anomalies between different socio-economic groups are also seen in statistical data researched in the UK. The incidence of premature death is not evenly spread throughout the population but is concentrated in the lower socio-economic group of society (see Figure 3.6). Unskilled workers, for example, run twice the risk of early death compared to professional people.

Often statistics raise more questions than they answer. For example, studies have shown that more people from the lower socio-economic group smoke cigarettes and

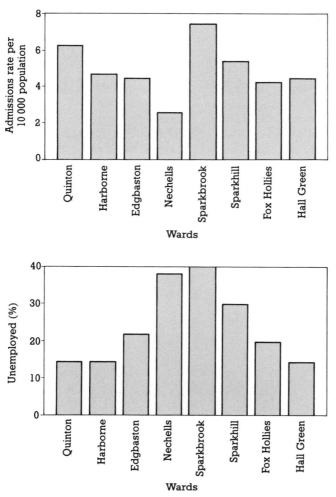

Figure 3.8   **a**   *Admissions for accidents at work (rate per 10 000 population) by ward for Central Birmingham, all ages*
    b   *Unemployment in Central Birmingham shown by ward, June 1986*

have no natural teeth, suggesting that health indicators, e.g. diet and smoking, may contribute to their higher rate of premature death. Professional people will be better educated and wealthier – are these important factors too? Longevity tends to be familial, i.e. the life span of parents and grandparents can be indicators for the life expectancy of an individual. There may be a genetic explanation for this or it may be because wealth, class and lifestyle are passed on to subsequent generations.

In the UK some of the areas of greatest deprivation are the inner city areas. A survey undertaken by the Central Birmingham Health Authority in 1987, 'A Picture of Health', encompassed both outlying and inner city areas, enabling useful comparisons (see Figure 3.7). The survey showed that the inner city areas were the worst affected in terms of illness and accident rates and they also had the highest unemployment and poorest housing conditions. One of the inner city areas, Sparkbrook, had the most accidents at work even though it had the highest unemployment rate (see Figure 3.8).

Premature deaths, from all causes, were higher in the inner city areas. The most common causes of death were heart disease, strokes, lung cancer, chronic lung disease, breast cancer and large bowel cancer.

Fewer elders live in the inner city than the outlying districts, but those living in the inner city are more likely to live alone (see Figures 3.9a and b). Although the number of ethnic elders is still fairly small (3 per cent) they are concentrated in inner city areas, so a high proportion of the older population in the inner cities will be black. The survey showed that two out of the three districts with the highest number of admissions of older adults to hospital are inner city areas (see Figure 3.10).

Ten per cent of admissions of elders to hospital are due to strokes and falls. Again people in the inner city areas are worst affected. As a higher proportion of these older people live alone, they may have to venture out in icy weather to get to the shops,

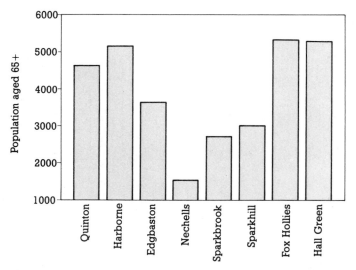

Figure 3.9   **a**   *Number of elderly people aged 65 and over in Central Birmingham , by ward*

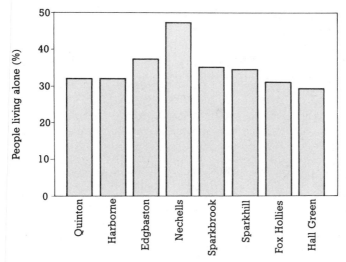

Figure 3.9 **b** *Percentage of elderly people aged 65 and over living alone, by ward*

resulting in falls, or they may be at home when they fall or have a stroke and lie undetected for some time before someone raises the alarm. In this case they may be admitted to hospital in a worsened condition, which will affect their eventual recovery and rehabilitation.

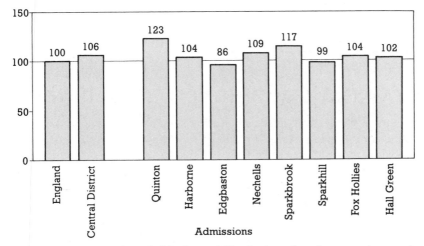

Figure 3.10 *Admissions to hospital in Central Birmingham for all causes by ward, ages 65 and over*

ACTIVITY

1 Look back at the figures used to present data for this chapter. Do you think that research which compares different groups of people by their socio-economic status, or by where they live, is productive?

2 Think about some positive reasons for conducting this sort of research, using examples from the text. Can you think of other ways of grouping people which might produce useful information? You might like to list the various factors used in the graphs in this chapter to start you off.

3 Are there any negative aspects to compiling data in this way? What action should follow the collection of this information? What recommendations would you suggest from the statistics shown in this chapter?

If you are studying the care of older people within a student group, you may find these points form an interesting discussion. Otherwise try to discuss your ideas with other carers.

Table 3.1 is a summary of the factors which will promote a long and healthy life, and the factors which will lead to premature ageing and early death.

Table 3.1   Factors for a long and healthy life and factors against

A long healthy life	Premature ageing and early death
Good diet	Poor diet and obesity
Genetic inheritance of longevity	Genetic inheritance of disease
Regular exercise	Lack of exercise
Good personal relationships	Loneliness and depression
Moderate wealth	Poverty and unemployment
Warm home	Poor housing
Leisure and recreation	Alcohol abuse and smoking
Good working conditions	Stress
Preventative health care	Overstretched primary health care team

MAINTAINING GOOD HEALTH IN OLD AGE

Old age is not a barrier to health and fitness – indeed health may be improved by changes in everyday living habits. Preparing for a healthy retirement really begins in childhood, when the seeds are sown for a healthy lifestyle. The chances of good health in old age are increased by good living earlier in life. However, it is never too late to start. The rules for healthy living apply to both sexes, all ages and all races and include the following points:

- *A good diet.* A well-balanced varied diet with lots of fresh fruit and vegetables (see page 50 for further details).
- *Not smoking.* Smoking damages health at all ages. Some older people believe that there is no point in giving up after many years because they feel that too much

damage has been done and 'they might as well enjoy it'. While it is true that irreversible changes will have taken place due to smoking, the benefits of giving up will always improve general health and breathing in particular.

- *Low alcohol consumption.* Alcohol taken in moderation is acceptable in maintaining good health. 'Moderation' can mean different things to different people; elders who are on medication or who suffer from certain conditions, may need to avoid alcohol altogether. It is sensible to seek advice from the family doctor on what is a reasonable amount for each individual.
- *Freedom from stress.* Freedom from all stress is neither possible nor desirable as stress can sometimes be quite beneficial. It can also be extremely harmful to the health of individuals if there is an unmanageable amount of stress in their lives. Older people are at a stage of life where they face many great changes and some inevitable losses. Carers need to support older people through these crises in order to counter the effects of the stress which bereavement, retirement, disability, illness and losing a family home may cause.
- *Relaxation and sleep.* The ability to relax is vital in dealing with stress. Elders will often find that they do not need as much sleep as they used to, perhaps because they lead a less active life and take naps during the daytime. It is better to try and find natural remedies for insomnia, e.g. having a milky drink at night, reading before going to bed and getting some fresh air in the day, rather than taking medication.
- *Exercise.* Exercise is essential for good health and fitness. Older people can counteract the effects of the ageing process by remaining active and keeping their bodies working. Exercise increases the intake of oxygen, improves the circulation and preserves mobility by strengthening muscles and joints. The amount and type of exercise that an elder can do will depend on their overall fitness and any underlying conditions they may have.
- *Loving relationships with family and friends.* This aspect of well-being was discussed in Chapter 2; Sullivan's research shows that good interpersonal relationships, between carers and clients, for example, are essential for a successful old age.
- *Stimulation.* Stimulation from a fulfilling occupation or leisure pursuit, and exercise, is important to keep older people physically and mentally active. Often a void can be felt by some people on retiring, particularly if they have always devoted themselves to their jobs. Older people should be encouraged to follow any pursuit which interests them.
- *A warm, damp-free, safe environment.* Older people need accommodation which provides this sort of environment. The ageing process leaves them more vulnerable to conditions such as hypothermia and bronchitis (see Chapter 4) and a warm home can offer protection from illness. The home should be a safe place, well-lit, secure and uncluttered, with well-maintained electrical equipment.

- *Fresh air and freedom from pollution.* Poorly ventilated air contains bacteria which are a source of infection. Elders should try to get out as much as possible and, if they have to remain indoors, they must make sure that the house is well-ventilated.
- *Personal hygiene.* This is necessary for maintaining good health and self-esteem. A daily bath or shower washes away dead skin cells and bacteria, maintaining the condition of the skin. Toe nails should be regularly attended to, ensuring that they do not grow too thick and long. Older people may suffer with dry skin and Afro-Caribbean people often have drier skin than white Europeans. Dry skin needs regular care in order to keep it supple and healthy. This can be achieved by adding a few drops of baby oil or olive oil to bath water or by applying a body lotion after bathing. Afro-Caribbean hair needs to be treated with oils and conditioners in order for it to remain supple and not become brittle and break.

WHAT IS A 'GOOD DIET'?

There are some general guidelines which people should follow to ensure a healthy diet. A good diet does not have to be expensive, and although it is difficult to manage on a pension, a well-balanced diet is possible.

A well-balanced diet should contain the following:

- Fresh fruit and vegetables to provide essential vitamins and fibre.
- Plenty of protein foods, which include soya products, a variety of pulses, dairy products, and meat and fish. These groups should be selected from according to personal custom and practice.
- Whole foods whenever possible, in order to obtain as much fibre in the diet as possible, e.g. wholemeal bread and pastry, brown rice and whole-wheat cereals.
- Not too much fat, particularly animal fat which contains cholesterol.
- Not too much sugar or sweet food (fats and sugar greatly increase the calorie content of the diet, contributing to obesity and heart disease).
- Not too much salt; excess salt is thought to contribute to high blood pressure.
- Plenty of water. Limit the intake of tea and coffee which both contain caffeine, a stimulant.
- Few highly processed foods, which contain additives and have lost much of their vitamin content, e.g. sweets, some tinned and dried foods, convenience meals, fizzy drinks. It is always worthwhile checking the contents of tins and packets for additives.

Reasons for a Bad Diet

The following list examines some of the factors which may contribute to older people neglecting their diet:

- *Low income.* Difficulty in managing on a pension.
- *Poor mobility.* Shops may be far away, and travelling may be difficult. If shops are close by, people may be hampered by a disability, e.g. breathlessness or arthritis.
- *Heavy shopping.* Fruit and vegetables are heavy to carry.
- *Physical effects of the ageing process.* Poor appetite and loss of taste or smell make eating less attractive.
- *Apathy and depression.* About 30 per cent of elders live on their own, and it may not seem worthwhile to prepare, cook and clear up for just one person, especially if the person is already depressed.
- *Ill-fitting dentures.* This makes meal-times a chore and encourages people to skip meals and to eat soft foods which are low in fibre.
- *Cold kitchen.* In the winter people may avoid spending a long time in the kitchen if they cannot afford to heat it.
- *Changing habits.* Poor eating habits acquired over the years may be difficult to change.

You can see, therefore, why someone might skip a meal and have a cup of tea and a biscuit instead; it is less expensive, less bother, no washing up and there is the feeling of 'Well, I wasn't hungry anyway'.

Overcoming Dietary Problems

Here are a few suggestions which elders may find useful.

- Have regular dental check-ups to ensure that existing teeth are healthy and that dentures fit well.
- If they live alone try to eat with others, perhaps taking it in turns to cook for a friend occasionally.
- Join local cookery classes or take different and unusual recipe books from the library to stimulate new ideas.
- Visit a local luncheon club, in order to socialise, eat a hot well-balanced meal and get out of the house.
- Visit day centres which also provide meals, and offer other support.
- Ask for Meals on Wheels to bring hot meals to the home if an elder cannot cook for themselves (there is a charge for this service).
- Ask if a home carer may be enlisted to do the shopping if shopping is difficult due to disability.

Changing the Diet

Encouraging people to make changes in their diets can be difficult as they often feel happiest with familiar favourites, or they may not be keen to experiment with new ways of cooking. It is much better to persuade people to make small changes, which they will be happy with, than to criticise their eating patterns. In this way they are more likely to 'have a go' and stick to the changes.

For people approaching retirement, advice can be given about diet in pre-retirement classes, e.g. how to cook well on a budget and how to prepare nutritional meals for one.

ACTIVITY

1 The following menus are from two older people. Read through both menus and say whether you think the diets of these elders are well-balanced.

2 What changes would you suggest? Give your reasons. Remember to suggest changes which you think would be acceptable to these older people. It is a good idea to have several alternatives that you could offer.

The recommendations which were suggested following discussion with the two elders are in Appendix 1, page 142. Compare them with your answers.

Mrs Smith
Mrs Smith is a widow who lives on her own in the house where she brought up her family. She has lost interest in cooking since the death of her husband but tries to look after herself properly. She suffers from constipation from time to time which she finds extremely uncomfortable and would like to alleviate this problem. This is a typical day's menu.

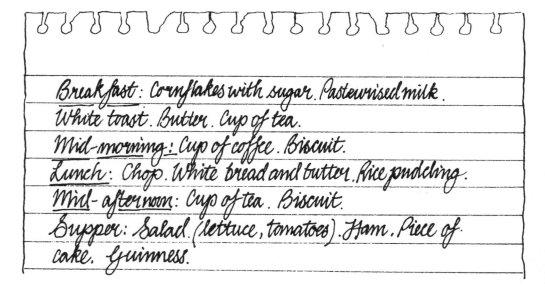

Breakfast: Cornflakes with sugar. Pasteurised milk. White toast. Butter. Cup of tea.
Mid-morning: Cup of coffee. Biscuit.
Lunch: Chop. White bread and butter. Rice pudding.
Mid-afternoon: Cup of tea. Biscuit.
Supper: Salad (lettuce, tomatoes). Ham. Piece of cake. Guinness.

Mr Richards

Mr Richards is a widower who also lives alone. He left Jamaica 30 years ago and can remember the abundance of fruit that filled the market place. Mr Richards is slightly overweight and suffers from arthritis. He has been told by his doctors that being overweight aggravates his condition.

This a typical day's menu.

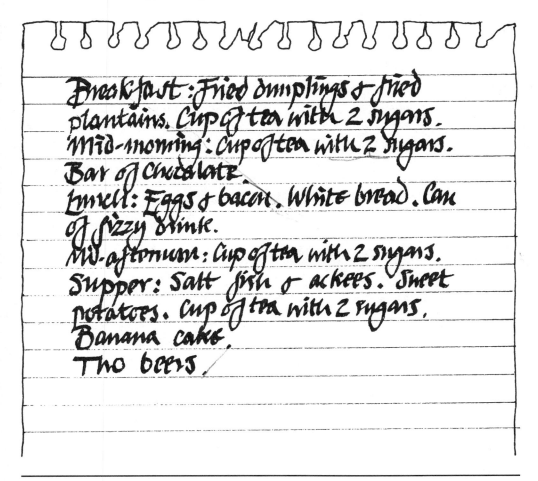

Breakfast: Fried dumplings & fried plantains. Cup of tea with 2 sugars.
Mid-morning: Cup of tea with 2 sugars. Bar of chocolate.
Lunch: Eggs & bacon. White bread. Can of fizzy drink.
Mid-afternoon: Cup of tea with 2 sugars.
Supper: Salt fish & ackees. Sweet potatoes. Cup of tea with 2 sugars. Banana cake. Two beers.

ASSIGNMENT 3   THE AGEING PROCESS

Research an aspect of the ageing process. You may like to explore the theories of ageing further or consider the effects of ageing on the body and practical strategies to counter this. You can do this as an in-depth case study on one older person or you may prefer to interview a selection of older people.

Remember to consider the experience of carers who have observed older people and have had to find solutions to specific problems. You may choose to interview a range of different carers and discuss their opinions. Read articles from journals and texts to supplement your investigation and try to find a piece of relevant research which has been undertaken on the aspect you have chosen.

If you are working in a group, present your project to your colleagues so that you can learn from each other's work.

Summary

Although there have been great improvements in the health and life expectancy of people this century, there are still large numbers of people whose life expectancy and rate of ageing is threatened by their living conditions and their lifestyle. Ageing is an inevitable process but ill health is not. However, it is sometimes difficult to separate ageing from ill health as ageing does not stand in isolation from the lives we lead and the times in which we live.

4 Old Age and Illness

In Chapter 3 you saw that ill health is not inevitable in old age but the incidence of it increases as the body cells wear out and are not replaced. Unfortunately, although people's life expectancy is far greater than ever before, not everyone who lives a long life enjoys good health. Many people have to learn to adapt themselves, their lifestyles and their environments in order to cope with diminishing strength, mobility and function caused by both **acute**, but more often **chronic** conditions.

In a 1987 *General Household Survey* sample 72 per cent of the people aged 75 and over had a long-standing illness, compared with 33 per cent of people of all ages. Fifty-eight per cent said that they had a long-standing illness which limited their lifestyle.

Many elders face difficulties adjusting to their own disability and loss of independence, as well as the stress which this imposes on their carers, whether this is a family member or a friend. A lifelong partner may be able to cope better emotionally with this increasing dependence, particularly if the relationship has been a mutually supportive one. However, the physical strain may prove detrimental to the health of the carer in the long run.

The following pages look at the importance of establishing the nature of the illness so that the right support can be offered to the sufferer and the carer.

DIAGNOSING ILLNESS

It is vital that a correct diagnosis is made when symptoms are presented so that appropriate treatment may be offered. While this should happen as a matter of course, unfortunately it is not always the case. There are several reasons why this does not happen, for example:

- Society expects older people to be infirm and this attitude pervades our thinking, influencing relatives, doctors, and the elders themselves.
- Older adults may put up with chronic long-term ailments because they wrongly assume that it is part of ageing and that there is nothing that can be done for them.
- Elders may not present their symptoms accurately due to embarrassment, confusion, or short-term memory loss.
- Doctors and other health practitioners may not always be able to give elders sufficient time in order to listen to them properly.
- There may be other communication difficulties due to cultural and class differences as well as problems with language, particularly if an appropriate interpreter cannot be found.

WHAT CARERS CAN DO

If an older adult is likely to need an interpreter, or may be forgetful about their symptoms, then their carer (or another appropriate person) should sit in on their consultation with the doctor. Carers can offer support by assisting the elder if necessary and by describing signs and symptoms which they have observed – for example, the mobility of a person – which can prove useful in aiding diagnosis and rehabilitation.

If an elder has a hearing aid the carer can make sure that the batteries are working and that it is switched on. If an older adult is likely to become confused in unfamiliar surroundings then carers can ask for a home visit. Sometimes if symptoms are worrying but too trivial to bother the doctor with, they can be discussed with the district nurse or the geriatric visitor, who can refer them to the doctor if necessary.

An older person who wishes to see their doctor on their own may find that writing a list of their symptoms and taking this with them helps them to remember everything that they wanted to say.

It may be beneficial for older adults to change their doctor, either within the practice or by going to another practice, where any of the following conditions apply:

- If an older adult prefers a doctor of the same sex.
- If there is a doctor available who can speak the same language as the elder.
- If another practice offers specialist facilities, for example, a practice nurse, a geriatric visitor or a well woman/man clinic.
- If the carer or the older person feels they would prefer someone with a more sympathetic approach.

Even if treatment cannot effect a cure, it may well be able to alleviate troublesome symptoms, which can transform the daily living of an older person. This may mean the difference between independence and dependence or between contentment and depression.

Sometimes an older adult is admitted to hospital so that their condition can be thoroughly assessed, but this is undertaken only if absolutely necessary as admission can sometimes disorientate or confuse an elder.

Older people, who are housebound or bedridden, may have their lives improved by nursing or physiotherapy techniques or by adaptations to their environment which can be recommended by an occupational therapist.

This chapter explores some illnesses and common ailments and considers suitable approaches to care.

ACTIVITY   Write down all the activities which you have to do every day in order to live. Sometimes it helps to ask other people what they think, so do this exercise with a colleague or someone at home. Your list might include:

- getting out of bed in the morning
- eating breakfast

- catching a bus
- ringing a friend
- making coffee

etc.

How many others can you think of?

When you have completed this, think about what it would mean for you if you could not perform any of these tasks for yourself. Imagine what it would feel like to be taken to the toilet and not to be able to wipe yourself clean. Look at the activities of daily living on your list and go through each one imagining your helplessness in each case. Write your feelings down and refer back to them as you read through this chapter.

CARING FOR DEPENDENT ELDERS

Chapter 1 looked at the different settings where we might care for older people and the qualities needed to be an effective carer. If you did the activity on page 17, about the qualities of carers, look back at your notes to refresh your memory. These qualities, when caring for dependent elders, will help you to offer a supportive and constructive caring environment. The following aims should be incorporated in your care regime:

- To enable the elders in your care to follow the cultural, dietary and religious practices which have been their normal way of life as closely as possible.
- To accommodate any life-long habits or practices into your care whenever possible and seek permission to change them if you consider it would be beneficial, for example, adapting clothing to make dressing easier.
- To work towards independence for older people giving them a choice about all aspects of their care, encouraging them to do as much as they can for themselves and respecting their decisions which you may disagree with.
- To be conscious at all times of an older person's need for privacy and respect, working to maintain their dignity and self-esteem.
- To **never** treat an elder as if they were a child, even if it is meant kindly.
- To make sure all physical needs, such as feeding, bathing, dressing, mobilisation and toileting are attended to, either by the elder with help or by the carer. Carers should ensure that pressure areas are cared for to prevent sores forming in people who are not very mobile.
- To provide a safe, warm, well-ventilated and cheerful environment.
- To ensure that they have enough sleep and rest and that their waking hours are filled with appropriate stimulation. Carers may be responsible for co-ordinating visitors, arranging for the loan of books or the purchase of wool for knitting. It is important to provide them with what they would like to do.
- To make time to listen to what elders are saying and to be approachable so that they feel able to disclose any little worries which they may have.
- To try and involve them when you are performing routine care tasks. Sometimes this can be difficult if they are demented or confused. It is acceptable to enter into their world or time zone in order to communicate, for example, talking about the times when the children were small.

COMMON CONDITIONS AND PHYSICAL ILLNESSES

Having established the correct approach to caring for dependent elders, the remainder of this chapter examines some of the commonest ailments and conditions which you will have to deal with, and the particular care and support you can offer.

HEART DISEASE

Heart disease is the biggest cause of death in the Western world. The effects of ageing and lifestyle on the blood vessels were discussed earlier (see page 37). When the arteries are badly damaged by atherosclerosis they become narrower and the likelihood of clots or debris blocking the passage of blood increases (see Figure 4.1).

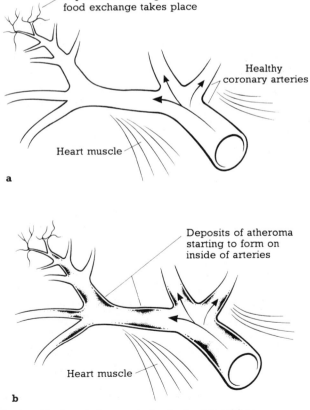

Figure 4.1   **a**   *The healthy heart. Arrows indicate the blood flow*
              b   *Atheroma is beginning to form*

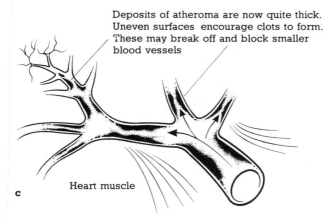

Deposits of atheroma are now quite thick.
Uneven surfaces encourage clots to form.
These may break off and block smaller
blood vessels

Heart muscle

c

c　*Diseased arteries. This person would be experiencing chest pain on exertion (angina). This is because the disease process has narrowed the blood vessels and is restricting blood flow*

Heart Attacks

A heart attack occurs when the blood supply to part of the heart muscle is cut off (see Figure 4.2). Unlike angina (see page 60), this often occurs when the person is resting. A very severe chest pain is experienced, often accompanied by sweating, breathlessness, dizziness and a grey pallor. There may be some cyanosis, which is blue tinges to the skin colour, especially around the lips and ear lobes. It should be noted that skin colour changes can be masked by dark pigmentation of the skin but the blue colour changes may be seen inside the mouth – you would need to open the mouth slightly to see.

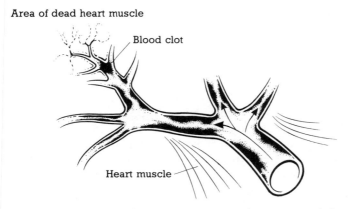

Area of dead heart muscle

Blood clot

Heart muscle

Figure 4.2　*A heart attack. A clot has formed in the lumen of a narrow and diseased arteriole. The blood cannot pass through and so the area of heart muscle which that vessel feeds will die. The person will experience great pain*

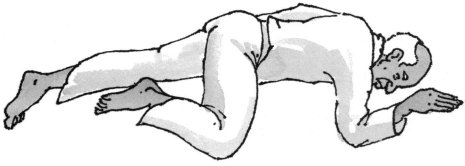

The recovery position

If you are with someone who has these symptoms, you should take the following action:

- Ask someone to call for an ambulance or, if you are on your own, do it yourself.
- If the person is conscious, support them in a sitting position with pillows or cushions if possible, as this will help their breathing.
- If the person is unconscious, lie on one side in the recovery position (above).
- Do not give them anything to drink, whether conscious or unconscious.
- Make sure they are as comfortable as you can make them and cover them with a blanket or coat to keep them warm.
- Stay with them until the ambulance arrives, remaining calm and reassuring.

The area of heart muscle which has been starved of oxygen by the lack of blood will die. The severity of the attack is in proportion to the size of the area which has been damaged and the position in which it takes place. For example, even if the area is small it may have a devastating effect if it is around the 'pace-maker' of the heart.

It is possible to make a full recovery from a heart attack following complete rest, medical and nursing care and a slow return to a balanced lifestyle, provided the damage to the heart is not too extensive.

Angina Pectoris

People with diseased coronary arteries may suffer from a condition called angina pectoris. This occurs when the heart's blood supply is insufficient for the demands made on it, due to the narrowed vessels. If sufferers exert themselves too much by exercising, or smoke, and the heart needs more blood than the arteries can provide, a severe pain is felt like a tight band across the chest, which often radiates down one or both arms or down the back.

The pain usually goes away fairly quickly if the person rests. There are drugs available which enlarge the blood vessels and these can be taken during an attack to speed the relief gained by resting. The severity and frequency of the attacks are related to the amount of **atheroma** in the arteries and to the amount of exertion.

Long-term treatment of this condition will depend on the age of the patient. It may affect younger people, who are sometimes advised to have surgery. Older people may not be suitable candidates for surgery and may need to rely on sensible living and medication. All sufferers may need to review their diets and lifestyles (see page 48).

Heart Failure

Heart failure is a condition which affects large numbers of elders. It is due to the heart becoming less efficient and not being able to pump blood around the body as effectively as it once could. It can be caused by coronary artery disease (as above) lung disease and high blood pressure. **Anaemia** and alcoholism may also be contributory factors.

Older adults who suffer from this condition often have excess fluid in their bodies which can make breathing difficult, particularly at night, and which causes their ankles to swell. Their ability to live normally can be curtailed by breathlessness, tiredness and lethargy. Fortunately drugs can be given both to reduce excess fluid by increasing the urinary output and to improve the heart's pumping action. This combination, while not effecting a cure, offers considerable relief and enables many sufferers to lead normal sedentary lives.

The carer's approach to heart disease should be to encourage a healthy diet with lots of fresh fruit and vegetables and not much fat. Medication should be taken regularly, exactly as prescribed. Elders should rest but they should not have complete bed rest unless directed by a doctor, as gentle mobility aids circulation and breathing, prevents pressure sores developing and keeps joints supple.

Carers may be able to compensate for the imposed inactivity of those suffering from this condition by ensuring that waking hours contain some stimulating experiences,

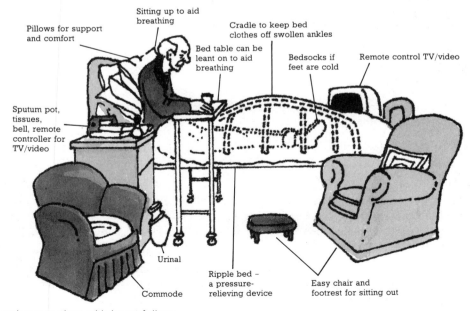

Nursing a patient with heart failure

such as an interesting activity or visitors, depending on the personal choice of the older adult.

Unfortunately some elders suffering from this condition live alone, dependent on the statutory caring services for their care in the community, and rely on personnel such as district nurses, home carers and social workers. This enforced isolation can be devastating to their morale and carers should seek to enlist the support of culturally appropriate local community volunteer groups in order to broaden the older person's world. Home visiting and good neighbour schemes would both be appropriate here.

LUNG DISEASES

The lung's air capacity diminishes with age but as an older person's demands are less this should not present too much of a problem. It is lung disease which incapacitates so many people and this is caused by infection, air pollution and smoking. It is made worse by the damp and cold weather.

Lung disease is a major cause of premature death, particularly in men, and it is also responsible for restricting the lives of many elders, disabling them through breathlessness. Smoking is the major cause of lung cancer but it is also responsible for weakening the lungs, making them susceptible to **bronchitis** and **emphysema**.

Lifelong smokers or others with lung damage often have the following problems:
● bronchitis – inflammation of the air passages
● emphysema – dilation of the air sacs
● bronchospasms – tightening of the air passages
● repeated lung infections over many years
● a perpetual cough
● producing sputum
● breathlessness, particularly following exertion (for example walking to the toilet).

STROKE

Although strokes are the second highest cause of premature death for both men and women, almost two-thirds of people who have a stroke will recover sufficiently to regain full independence.

A stroke is caused by an area of the brain having its blood supply cut off either by a blood clot or an **embolus**, or by a **haemorrhage**. A stroke is similar to a heart attack, in that it is the result of diseased blood vessels which have been narrowed by atheroma.

The severity of the stroke will depend on the size of the area affected by the loss of blood supply and also on the function which that area of brain co-ordinates. A stroke can occur anywhere within the brain and the symptoms vary according to where the damage has taken place.

If the stroke is very severe the patient may go into a coma and die. Most patients, however, do not die but they are left disabled in some way and full recovery often takes a long time. The patients most likely to do well are those who can develop and maintain a positive attitude towards their situation. This is often hampered by the

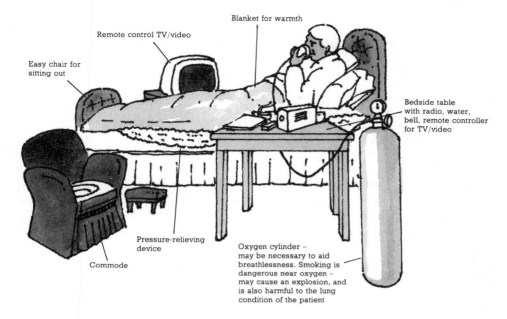

Easy chair for
sitting out

Remote control TV/video

Blanket for warmth

Bedside table
with radio, water,
bell, remote controller
for TV/video

Pressure-relieving
device

Commode

Oxygen cylinder –
may be necessary to aid
breathlessness. Smoking is
dangerous near oxygen –
may cause an explosion, and
is also harmful to the lung
condition of the patient

Nursing a patient with lung disease

effect that the stroke has on their emotional state, making them excessively tearful and depressed.

Older people who have suffered a stroke may need to relearn basic tasks and functions, e.g. walking unaided, speaking, dressing, bathing, and cooking. In hospitals the occupational therapists will work out a programme of rehabilitation in consultation with other members of the caring team.

It is important that all those caring for the stroke patient, whether relatives, professionals or volunteers, try to encourage the older person to do as much as possible for themselves. Carers should have realistic goals for the elder to achieve and be optimistic, patient, reassuring and willing to give them their time.

This is a bewildering condition for any elder but it can be terrifying for older adults who cannot speak English well, if at all. A speech therapist who has no knowledge of Asian languages will not be able to offer much help, even with the aid of an interpreter. Older people who have learnt English as a second language may revert back to their heritage language following the shock of their stroke. Without appropriate cultural support these elders will have an additional burden which can only impede their recovery, and carers should make every effort to provide that support.

Physical Effects of a Stroke

- *Speech*. Speech can be affected in several ways. Words may be slurred and difficult to understand or they may be totally out of context because the connection between the choice of a word and its being spoken is damaged. The patient is aware of this and is usually very distressed by it.

- *Emotions.* Elders may either laugh inappropriately or be very tearful, negative and depressed. They may experience mood swings.
- *Walking and balance.* One side of the body is usually affected by a stroke and elders may be able to be mobile with help, a stick or a walking frame. Elders may need support until their balance is regained.
- *Movement.* There may be paralysis down one side of the body, affecting the arm or leg or both. This makes independent living difficult. Patients need physiotherapy to help them regain the use of their bodies.
- *Sensory perception.* Elders may not feel cold, heat, pain or touch on the affected side.
- *Elimination.* Sufferers may become incontinent. A rehabilitation programme can be undertaken to promote continence. This is discussed in more detail later (see page 65).
- *Swallowing.* Swallowing may be affected. Care needs to be taken so that patients do not choke on their food.
- *Vision.* Vision may be impaired, causing further bewilderment to sufferers.

PREVENTION OF PRESSURE SORES

It is important to mention pressure area care in this chapter because it is a vital aspect of caring for patients who are not fully mobile. When people lose their mobility they apply greater pressure on parts of their skin than they would normally do if they could walk about freely. The vulnerable areas are those which are near bony parts of the body (see below).

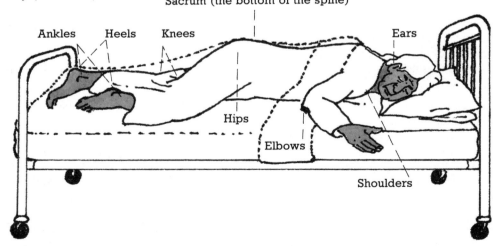

Areas of the body which are vulnerable to pressure sores

Pressure area care requires patients to be turned (or stood up if they are sitting out of bed) at least every two hours, even if they are only slightly immobile, so that the pressure on the skin can be released. Failure to do this will result in pressure sores forming. Once these occur it is difficult to heal them and they can easily become infected, contributing to the death of a debilitated patient.

Some people are more vulnerable than others to pressure sores, particularly if they:

- are an older adult
- have poor nutrition (lack of protein and vitamin C will affect healing)
- are incontinent (especially if they are allowed to lie in a wet bed for any length of time)
- have crumpled bed sheets, which may cause uneven pressure
- are over- or under-weight
- have any small abrasions in the skin (caused by scraping the skin when getting a patient off a bed pan, for example).

Carers should ask for nursing advice when trying to prevent pressure sores. If a pressure sore occurs it is a serious development and should always be supervised by a health professional.

INCONTINENCE

Incontinence affects about 40 per cent of very old people, but is common amongst older people generally and affects people of all ages as well. It is a condition which can be the source of both daily irritation and deep humiliation to its sufferers and requires sensitive and intelligent management.

We have all been incontinent of both urine and faeces when we were babies. In becoming continent we had to reach several developmental milestones. These were mobility, communication, awareness of full bladder and bowel sensation, the ability to retain urine and faeces till elimination was appropriate and the understanding of socially acceptable behaviour.

Continence, i.e. having control over your body's elimination, is still dependent on a multiplicity of factors, some of which can be easily remedied.

It will be helpful at this point to explore some of the effects of ageing on the lower urinary tract:

- As people age their bladder capacity diminishes, increasing the frequency of urination. Older people often have to get up at night to go to the toilet.
- The bladder is less able to empty completely and often holds residual urine of about a fifth of a pint, encouraging infection, particularly if an elder is not drinking very much.
- The awareness of a full bladder is less sensitive. A younger person is alerted by the nervous system when the bladder is only half full and so has more time to choose when to urinate.
- Childbirth can weaken the pelvic floor muscles and can lead to the leakage of urine when abdominal pressure is increased, e.g. when coughing or laughing (this is known as stress incontinence).
- The prostate gland can become a problem for men. It is common for it to become enlarged as they grow older, which may eventually result in retention of urine, needing surgical treatment. It can also lead to dribbling incontinence, where small amounts of urine continuously leak.

Older people need to go to the toilet more frequently and more urgently than younger people and are more likely to find it an arduous task, sometimes an impossible one. A vicious circle can develop, whereby an older adult restricts their fluid intake in order not to need the toilet (often this is done not to bother the carer) which in turn increases the risk of urine infection. Frequency and urgency are both worsened by infection, which can be extremely uncomfortable and requires an increased consumption of fluids as part of the treatment.

Some Reasons for Not Drinking

- 'Oh dear – I wet the bed last night – I'd better do without'
- 'I can't reach it.'
- 'I'll only spill it.'
- 'I don't like the tea without sugar.'
- 'I don't want to bother the nurse for the pan – I've only just been.'
- 'It's too hot.'
- 'I don't want to call the nurses during the night/while they're busy.'
- 'They get cross if you keep ringing the bell.'

Some Reasons for Incontinence

- Arthritic fingers may find buttons and other fastenings difficult to undo in a hurry.
- Stairs to the toilet may take a long time to climb.
- An elder may forget where the toilet is in an unfamiliar place such as a hospital or a home, especially if signs are inadequate or in another language.
- The toilet seat may be too low for a disabled person.
- Communicating the need to go to the toilet may be affected by not speaking the same language as carers, by deafness, or by speech difficulties caused by strokes and short-term memory loss.

Prevention is better than cure, so it is prudent to provide older people with the means to toilet themselves easily or with as little assistance as possible from a carer, by, for example:

- altering the fastenings on garments from buttons and hooks to velcrose
- fitting rails in the toilet and a raised toilet seat or putting a commode in the bedroom at night
- considering surgical repair, such as to a prolapsed uterus, which may provide the cure for an existing condition
- making access to the toilet as easy as possible. It is the carer's responsibility to enable their clients to eliminate as soon as they have expressed a wish to do so.

Managing Permanent Incontinence

For those older adults with established incontinence there are a wide range of aids, which are available free from the community nursing service, for example:

- Washable pants with a disposable pad inserted into the pocket (a).
- Disposable pants with the pad sewn in (b).

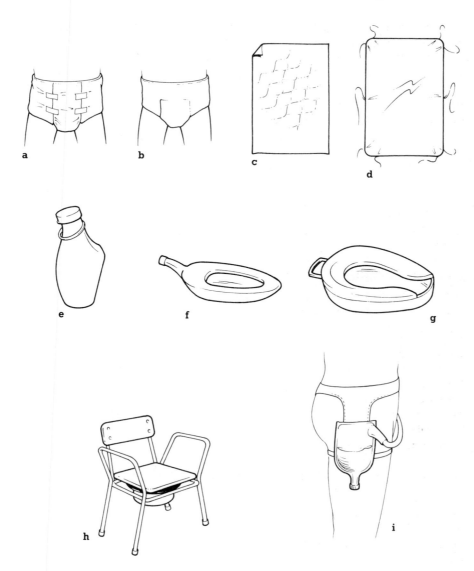

- Kylie bed sheet which absorbs water (c).
- Linen and plastic draw sheets to protect the bed linen (d).
- Urinal to enable men to urinate without getting out of bed or out of a chair (e).
- Feminal, for women to urinate without getting up; can be attached to a bag (f).
- Bedpan for patients who cannot get out of bed to go to the toilet (g).
- Commode – a toilet, usually on wheels, often designed to look like an ordinary chair which can be kept in the bedroom (h).
- Catheter – a tube attached to a bag is inserted into the bladder by a nurse or doctor (i). The bag can be emptied by carers or by elders themselves. Catheterisation can give relief from the embarrassment of incontinence and from the trauma of toileting an ill patient. Long-term use is discouraged as the catheter encourages bacteria and increases the risk of infection.

The continence advisor (a district nursing sister with specialist knowledge) would be the best person to advise an older person on the most appropriate way for them to manage their incontinence. Part of this management may include a toilet training regime, which would be discussed with those caring directly for the elder. This is a programme in which the older person visits the toilet every two hours, including through the night, in order to empty the bladder before it becomes too full. It is often carried out in hospitals and homes as part of a rehabilitation process. In toilet training timing is vital and the success of the programme rests with the ability of the staff to implement it consistently.

ARTHRITIS

There are two types of arthritis: rheumatoid arthritis and osteoarthritis.

Rheumatoid Arthritis

Rheumatoid arthritis affects people of all ages but usually starts when someone reaches middle age. It is thought to be an allergic response by the body which affects the whole system and the joints in particular. Joints become swollen and inflamed during an attack.

Caring for rheumatoid arthritis sufferers in the acute phase involves:

- Rest: affected joints are rested and may be splinted. A cradle may be used if leg joints are affected.
- Medication as prescribed – usually pain-killers and anti-inflammatory drugs.
- Plenty of nourishing fluids high in calcium, e.g. milk.

Following the acute phase:

- Exercise and heat therapy to affected joints, supervised by the physiotherapist.

Osteoarthritis

Osteoarthritis is a more common condition; some arthritic changes will be present in the joints of most older people, even if they are not aware of any symptoms. It is a diseased state caused by the wearing out of the cartilage which surrounds the joints and is therefore more likely to affect the joints which have worked hardest throughout a lifetime, e.g. the weight bearing joints, such as the hip and the knees, and the smaller ones in the hand, especially the first finger and thumb.

The joints stiffen and become painful to move as the ends of the bones lose their protection. Nodules may appear and the disease process often causes deformity to the joint, restricting movement further. This can impede daily activities drastically, particularly if the condition is severe enough to make movement painful, clumsy or even impossible.

If the arthritis is in the hip or knee joint the elder may become virtually house-bound, living constantly with pain, dependent on others for shopping and possibly dressing and bathing too. If the affected joints are in the hands then tasks which require dexterous fingers, e.g. doing up buttons, holding cutlery, will become difficult and frustrating and, in some cases, impossible.

An affected hip joint can be replaced by surgery; this is the only way that the condition can be cured. Unfortunately people often have to wait a long time for the operation, or there may be medical reasons why surgery should not be performed.

The approach to caring for an older person with this chronic illness should be positive and imaginative. If an activity is no longer easy for them to do then the following questions should be asked:

- Is it easier to do it another way?
- Is it necessary to do it at all?
- Can something else be done instead?
- Can the immediate environment be adapted so that it can be done?
- Is there a device available which may help?
- Is it possible to seek help and advice from those with knowledge in the field, either fellow sufferers and carers or professionals?

It is important to try and have a positive approach so that depression about their condition does not increase their disability. There are a wide range of aids available which can enable them to be independent.

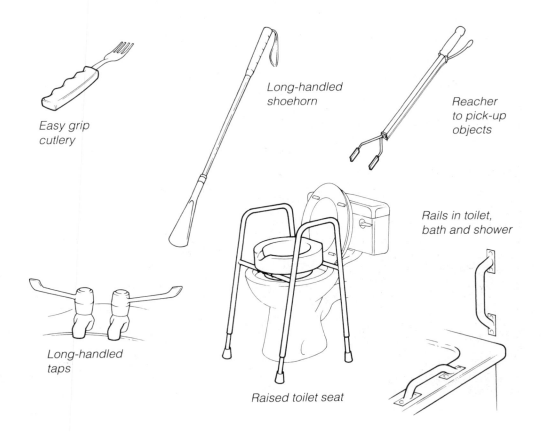

Easy grip cutlery

Long-handled shoehorn

Reacher to pick-up objects

Long-handled taps

Raised toilet seat

Rails in toilet, bath and shower

Large handles
on plugs

Velcrose and
zip pullers

Elastic tie
and laces

Photograph courtesy of Stannah Stairlifts Limited

Some local authorities provide a service whereby an occupational therapist will visit older adults in their homes and advise them on appropriate aids. There may be a Disabled Living Centre which an elder can visit themselves where they can try out various aids and be advised on what is most suitable.

VISUAL IMPAIRMENT

The lens of the eye becomes less elastic with age and this will cause changes in visual acuity, i.e. clear focusing ability. Glasses are usually sufficient to correct this and it is essential for older adults to have their eyes tested regularly by an optician. Those people who have never needed spectacles may now require them and those who already wear them may need their lenses changing.

Visual impairment in older people may also be due to diseases of the eye. A common condition is cataracts, where the lens of one or both eyes gradually becomes cloudy, causing increasing loss of visual ability. Correct diagnosis and treatment is important, as the appropriate lenses will help and surgical treatment is also possible.

Carers can help by making sure the home is well-lit and that there are extra lights for reading or knitting. A night light in the bedroom may be useful and a light left on in the hall at night will enable an older person to go to the toilet safely.

If an older person's sight is severely impaired, practical support may be necessary for all basic living tasks. Emotional support may also be needed, as it is a bewildering and frightening experience.

An occupational therapist can visit the older person in their home to advise on any aids which might be useful, e.g. a magnifying glass with a light attached, or elastic shoe laces which do not need to be tied.

The local library can provide large print books, cassettes of 'talking' books and sometimes musical records and tapes. Small rural libraries which may not stock these items can often borrow them for you. The local branch of the Royal National Institute for the Blind will be able to offer support to both sufferers and carers.

HEARING IMPAIRMENT

Gradual hearing loss is common in older adults and it is important to seek medical advice if an older person becomes hard of hearing (sometimes carers are more aware of this than the older person, especially if there is a gradual decline). The ears may simply need washing out, or a hearing aid may give the wearer improved hearing.

If an older person has difficulty in hearing, sit close to them when you are talking to them and face them so they can see your face clearly. Talk normally and if you need to repeat things, take your time and do not show exasperation. Make an effort to include the person in conversation as elders may withdraw through lack of contact.

Safety in the home needs to be reassessed and the occupational therapist may be able to make helpful suggestions. Special care needs to be taken on the roads as traffic will be less easily heard.

DIABETES

Diabetes mellitus is an illness caused by an absence or a deficiency of insulin. Insulin is the enzyme responsible for the entry of glucose into the cells and is therefore essential for cell metabolism. There are two types of diabetes mellitus. The first is a total absence of insulin, which most commonly occurs when people are still young and is treated by a daily injection of insulin. The second is due to the pancreas producing insufficient insulin for the body's needs. The onset of this disease usually occurs around middle age and the treatment consists of a combination of oral medication to stimulate the pancreas and rationing carbohydrates in the diet.

The cause of this type of diabetes may be due in part to the effects of ageing on the pancreas, but a high sugar diet and being overweight are also contributory factors.

Diabetes increases the likelihood of vascular disease and affects the healing process. Diabetics should have regular eye tests as damage to the retina is a further complication, and they should visit the chiropodist regularly.

HYPOTHERMIA

When the body temperature falls below 35°C hypothermia sets in. This could happen to young healthy adults exposed for long periods in extreme cold and adverse conditions. In older people a low grade hypothermia is more commonly caused by sitting around in under-heated homes or coming in from the cold into a chilly house. Severe hypothermia, which may be caused by an elder lying on a cold floor all night unable to move, due to a fall perhaps, can result in coma and later death.

Older adults' heat regulating mechanisms are not able to cope very well with changes in temperature, especially in maintaining body warmth. They may also generate less heat from their bodies than younger people if they are less mobile, either due to having less to do or because of a medical condition which restricts movement, for example, arthritis or lung disease.

More older people die in the winter than in the summer. Most of these deaths are not directly caused by hypothermia (though some are) but the lowered body temperature of some elders living at home is thought to contribute to this higher winter death rate. It has been estimated that there are 8000 'excess deaths' for every degree celsius the winter is colder than average.

Prevention of hypothermia involves highly practical and relatively simple measures. If you are caring for an older person living in their own home you may find the following suggestions helpful:

- Ensure a room temperature of 20 °C minimum – suggest a room thermometer to check this.
- Encourage several layers of light, warm clothing rather than one large, heavy item.
- Ensure frequent nourishing, warm drinks (possibly kept nearby in a handy flask).
- Encourage mobility as light exercise will generate internal heat.
- Ensure a warmed bedroom and a warm bed; an electric blanket is ideal provided it is switched off when the elder gets into bed.
- Check the room for draughts and ensure doors and windows are draught-proof.

- A personal alarm in case of falls for elders living alone.
- If the property is too expensive to heat adequately or is in need of repair, advice should be sought about heating allowances, local authority grants or alternative accommodation.

If you find someone whom you suspect may be suffering from hypothermia do not rely on an ordinary thermometer, which will not register below 35°C. Seek medical help and while you are waiting heat the room and cover the person with a blanket. It is important not to warm up someone suffering from hypothermia too quickly as this can be dangerous. Never use a hot water bottle. A warm, milky drink would be beneficial unless the person has collapsed and is unconscious, in which case do not give them a drink, as the swallowing reflex is lost and the person will choke.

ACTIVITY

Imagine that you are working as an auxiliary nurse with the community nursing service. One of your regular patients is an elderly Polish man who is recovering from a stroke and who needs 24-hour nursing support, most of which is provided by his wife with your daily help. Although he could speak English before his stroke, he has reverted to speaking Polish.

He is suffering from dysarthia which means he is slurring his words and even his wife, who speaks Polish, finds him difficult to understand. He had hemiplegia, i.e. paralysis down one side of the body; but this is now sufficiently improved for him to walk with the aid of a frame. He needs help with bathing, toileting and feeding.

The couple have a daughter who calls in twice weekly (who cannot speak any Polish) and several friends from the local Polish community.

1 Outline and prioritise the main care tasks the patient and his family need help with.

2 Devise a plan of action showing how you would tackle these tasks. Indicate on this plan what you would do yourself and what support you would seek from colleagues.

3 Discuss your plan with colleagues. Add any further ideas or potential problems which these discussions may have raised.

A suggested answer may be found in Appendix 1, page 143.

Summary

The common conditions which affect older people and the various caring approaches needed have been considered in this chapter. Remember that not all elders suffer with these ailments and there are many other, less common, conditions which you may come across. The caring approaches to any condition have many similarities, however, including the need to listen properly, to promote independence, to provide the elder with choices and to be patient.

Arm yourself with as much information as you can about the condition of the elder in your care. You should ask other carers about their experiences and you should listen to the elders themselves. If you have a good idea for improving care and making life easier – suggest it.

⑤ Old Age and Mental Infirmity

The previous chapter concentrated on the common physical ailments which affect elders. This chapter looks at the mental disorders which older people may be prone to. The incidence of mental disorders in old age is difficult to ascertain exactly as research in this area is complex and sometimes evidence is conflicting. The three most common conditions are confusion, depression and senile dementia.

MENTAL HEALTH IN OLD AGE

The effects of ageing and of vascular disease on the brain were considered in Chapter 4. The main points are outlined again here, to refresh your memory:

- The cells which make up the nervous system are called neurones, and we lose 10 000 neurones a day from about the age of 25.
- The speed at which messages are transmitted along the neurones decreases by about 10 per cent as we age.
- Short-term memory recall (remembering what happened very recently) becomes less efficient.
- Long-term memory (e.g. memories of childhood) remains clear.
- Learning new skills may be more difficult as co-ordination and memory affect learning ability.
- Atherosclerosis of the arteries which supply the brain with blood can lead to strokes.

It is important to bear in mind the following facts:

- Intelligence is not impaired by the loss of brain cells.
- Learning ability can be improved by motivation and experience.
- Diminished intellectual ability is caused by mental and physical illness and can be either temporary or permanent.

ATTITUDES AND STEREOTYPING

Stereotyping, and its insidious effects on older people, was considered in Chapter 1. Do you think it has any relevance here? Consider the following summary of Open University examination results.

> Academically, over-60s students at the OU have a slightly lower drop-out rate than the under-60s, do slightly better in continuous assessment, but slightly worse in examinations. The overall pass rate is similar for all ages and in terms of pass rate, those aged 60 to 64 are among the most successful of OU students.
>
> Clennell *et al.*, 1984

Are you surprised by the fact that most successful students are those aged between 60 and 64? If you are, is that because your unconscious perception of older people is that they are intellectually less able than younger people? It is not the purpose of this book to make you feel guilty about these perceptions but rather to make you aware of them. This attitude is not new, nor is the awareness of ageism. Samuel Johnson (1709–84) wrote the following:

> There is a wicked inclination in most people to suppose an old man decayed in his intellects. If a young or middle-aged man, when leaving a company, does not recollect where he laid his hat, it is nothing; but if the same inattention is discovered in an old man, people will shrug up their shoulders, and say, 'His memory is going'.

The stereotype of the forgetful elder has a strong and forceful image which, like all stereotypes, is based on some fact, as the working, everyday memory becomes less efficient with age. However, as people grow older they acquire more skills to aid their memory, for example:

- using a diary for appointments
- writing 'things to be done' lists
- writing shopping lists
- making use of alarms on clocks and watches
- asking others to remind them
- leaving memos to themselves and others in prominent places as reminders.

Do you use any of these memory aids? When revising for an exam you may have been taught to use rhymes, repetition, first-letter association or other methods to aid recall, not because it was feared that you may be becoming senile but because there is a huge variation between people of all ages in their ability to remember things, and nobody, whether young or old, has a perfectly efficient memory.

Some elders may be so worried by the possibility of becoming senile that they may perceive themselves as becoming more forgetful than is actually the case. If the list of memory aids had been written in a book about effective time-management for busy young executives, do you think that it would have been viewed differently than if it had appeared in a self-help manual for older people?

CONFUSION

Have you ever been lost? As a child you may have been separated from your parents for a short time, finding yourself alone in a strange place. Can you recall your feelings? You may have felt irrational panic, strangers may have appeared threatening and the crowds or the darkness may have become terrifyingly oppressive. And then, thankfully, you recognised where you were or spotted a familiar face, and felt your heartbeat returning to normal. These feelings are similar to those experienced by elders in an acute confusional state although returning to an awareness of reality and normality is not always so easily achieved.

Confusional states can be acute or chronic, but they are reversible and can be treated. If untreated, they can unfortunately, become permanent. Older people are doubly disadvantaged if they become confused and forgetful because so many people (including carers, professionals and the elders themselves) regard this as an inevitable part of the ageing process. This may prevent a proper diagnosis of the problem, effective treatment and a resolution to the confused state.

CAUSES OF CONFUSION

Confusion is a malfunction of a healthy brain in response to one of three causes:

1 A response to a physical illness, for example, heart attack, heart failure, lung disease (bronchitis or pneumonia) and strokes. It can also be caused by myxoedema (a thyroid gland deficiency) or vitamin B12 deficiency. Any physical illness may bring on a state of confusion.

2 Medication which the elder has been prescribed. This should always be reviewed if an acute confusional state occurs. Older people generally need smaller doses of drugs, as they tend to remain in the body for longer periods.

3 A response to a change of environment or an emotional trauma. This could be the death of a spouse or a close friend, going into hospital, moving into residential accommodation or moving in with a daughter or son's family.

SIGNS AND SYMPTOMS OF CONFUSION

The signs and symptoms of confusion are complex. You may notice the following changes in behaviour of older adults:

- communication may be difficult; the person may talk inappropriately and out of context
- periods of drowsiness and poor concentration
- disorientation, not knowing where they are, or what day or time it is
- restlessness, twitching and wandering
- misinterpretation of their environment; shadows or objects can become animals, people, long-dead relatives, etc. causing fear and terror, similar to the feelings experienced by a lost child.

TREATMENT AND CARING APPROACH

If the cause of the confusional state is a response to a physical illness, or prescribed drugs, the treatment is relatively straightforward. The physical illness may be treated and stabilised, if not cured, and the confusion should go. Medication should be reviewed, and either alternative drugs prescribed, or medication may be stopped altogether.

The third cause of confusion, a change of environment or an emotional trauma, is more difficult to treat because its cause is not so easily remedied. For instance, an older woman admitted to a residential home because she is frail and her own accommodation is inadequately heated and unsuitable will find her new environment strange and unfamiliar, with no 'memory tags' for her to use.

Some helpful approaches which may be employed in this case are illustrated below but it must be emphasised that this is an extremely difficult nursing task that requires

patience, resilience and compassion. The following aids may help the carer and the patient:

- familiar knick-knacks, objects, furniture and clothes from home
- doors labelled with illustrations and names to prevent people from getting lost (in hospitals these names should be in all the languages of the local communities)
- speaking clearly and slowly, repeating important information without being patronising, and ensuring that there is someone available who can interpret if necessary
- pictorial calendars and clocks in prominent places
- reality orientation therapy (see below) – in specific sessions and as part of the nursing care.

Staff should be calm and reassuring whenever necessary. It may also help if, before an elder is admitted to a home, they have a period of acclimatisation, in the form of a weekend or even a two-week stay, in order to get used to the new environment. If the process is unhurried, with the elder's full consent, then there is more chance of a problem-free transition.

Reality Orientation Therapy

Reality orientation therapy (ROT) is an increasingly popular activity for both staff and older people in homes and day centres. Its aim is to provide elders with a sense of reality and encourage social interaction which may otherwise be lost due to the following factors:

- short-term memory loss
- a similar routine every day, with nothing to make a day special or different
- loss of conversation skills from living alone or being with others who are confused, have a speech or hearing disability or who speak another language.

ROT can bring people in touch with reality, reminding them what day it is and what is happening around them. It can also promote conversation skills by encouraging people to talk about their memories. Often people have things in common, particularly if they have lived in the locality all their lives, giving them something to share and talk about. Memories need to be jogged and pictures, old photographs and objects from their youth may help.

ROT sessions are arranged in small groups. It is important to use people's names and, if necessary, to repeat what has been said so that everyone can become involved and participate fully in the session.

An ethnic elder in the group may have spent his or her childhood and early adult life in a different country and may not be able to share common memories with the others in the group (for example, going to the local school, wartime experiences) and old photographs of the locality will not help to jog their memory. This can be overcome if special units in sheltered or residential accommodation are created for people of a similar cultural background. This is explored further in Chapter 7. It would be useful to find out about the country of an ethnic elder's birth so that relevant photographs may be obtained. Libraries and ethnic minority associations may be able to help with this.

For those elders who have either reverted to their heritage language or who have never learnt to speak English, it is vital that they have someone to converse with in the language which they speak. Stringent efforts should be made to recruit appropriate staff and residents but in the meantime local community groups may be able to provide visitors who can communicate in the particular language spoken.

Inevitably wartime experiences may surface from time to time as the war was a major event in people's lives. It is important to be aware that individuals' experiences of the war may be very different and that for some people memories will be more painful than for others. While two older people may chat about shared good times in air raid shelters another person may have been a prisoner of war and experienced terrible hardship. The process of retracing any memories needs to be handled with care, sensitivity and discretion.

CASE STUDY   *Dora Baker*

Dora Baker was an 85-year-old widow living alone in her own home. She was a little unsteady on her feet and took medi- cation for slight heart failure but was otherwise in good health and managed very well. Her son visited her once or

twice a month, she had the home carer in once a week and she attended a luncheon club three days a week.

One cold January morning Dora set out for the shops for some groceries. She had not ventured out the previous week because it had snowed and so she was low on essential foods. The luncheon club was not until tomorrow and Becky, the home carer, would not be in for a couple of days. Unfortunately ice had formed on the pavements and Dora lost her balance, fell awkwardly and broke her leg. Dora was taken to St Swithuns hospital, a large Victorian institution which Dora could remember when it was the workhouse. She was admitted to a

busy female orthopaedic ward, taken to the operating theatre, where a pin and plate were secured on to the broken bone. Dora was returned to the ward, and was in a lot of pain. She was very confused and kept insisting on seeing her husband who had been dead for 15 years.

She kept others awake at night by shouting so the doctor prescribed sleeping tablets for her. These did not prove effective until the early hours of the morning which meant that Dora remained awake through the night and slept during the day. The nurses put up cot sides at night so that Dora would not fall out of bed and hurt herself, which meant she could not get out to go to the toilet and was too confused to ring her bell, and so became incontinent. As Dora often slept for most of the day she was not receiving enough to drink. This added to her confused state, and she also developed a urinary tract infection.

The loss of mobility and her sleepy state meant that Dora developed pressure sores which soon became infected due to her incontinence.

Dora's son visited his mother and was shocked to find her so poorly. She had been a highly independent, sharp-witted old lady and now she was incontinent, completely dependent and totally confused.

Although this is a frightening picture of spiralling events, unfortunately it is not uncommon. It is not always possible to prepare people for admission into strange surroundings. What do we do about emergencies?

ACTIVITY 1

Read through the case study again and then answer the following questions.

1 Describe in your own words what happened to Dora and why you think her condition deteriorated.
2 List the nursing problems which exist now.
3 How would you suggest the whole caring team should approach these problems?
4 How might this catalogue of events have been prevented?

Suggested answers to these questions can be found in Appendix 1, pages 144–5.

DEPRESSION

Depression is a word often used – 'My boyfriend's just finished with me, I haven't a hope of passing these exams and I'll never get a job the way things are . . . I'm so depressed.' These feelings are not trivial but generally they are part of life and we learn to deal with them reasonably well. Sometimes depression can be prolonged and relentless and can affect our mental and physical health. In this case it should be viewed as an illness, thoroughly investigated and appropriate treatment prescribed.

Depression can be a mild, moderate or a severe condition. It can be reactive, i.e. a response to a traumatic event such as the death of a spouse. Or it can be endogenous, i.e. there is no apparent reason in the sufferer's life for these feelings. Depression is a fairly common condition, suffered by 8 to 14 per cent of people over the age of 65. Suicide rates are higher for older adults, particularly men, than for any other age group. Younger people attempt suicide more frequently but use less serious means and are less likely to be successful.

If some or all of the following signs and symptoms are experienced by elders over a period of weeks, then their condition should be a cause for concern and medical help should be sought:

- feelings of guilt, low self-esteem and a sense of worthlessness
- loss of appetite
- loss of libido, i.e. interest in sex (although this might only become apparent in situations where there has been a previously satisfactory sex life with a partner)
- feelings of tiredness
- weight loss (or weight gain, less common in older people)
- insomnia
- loss of pleasure and interest in previously enjoyed hobbies
- slowing of speech, poor concentration
- hypochondria
- constipation
- delusions
- suicidal thoughts.

It is normal to feel depressed following loss, whether that loss is the death of a loved one or the loss of a family home after moving into residential accommodation. It may be the loss of a way of life, for example, retirement or becoming disabled, which causes the depression.

Everyone needs to grieve in order to work through their sadness and come to terms with their loss (this is discussed in more detail in Chapter 8). The grieving process can become more difficult if it is complicated by other factors, such as loneliness, physical illness or moving from familiar surroundings, and it can become prolonged, resulting in a depressive state.

Carers need to be aware of this and to be sensitive to changes in an older person's mood and behaviour. They should work at prevention of a depressive state by supporting and counselling elders through any form of loss and by making change as easy as possible. Carers working in residential homes need to appreciate that their clients may have become depressed before they came into the home. Changes in personality and behaviour may have already occurred. If there are any worrying symptoms, staff could ask family or friends if they have observed changes.

TREATMENT AND CARE

The treatment of depression will depend on the type and cause of the illness and the circumstances of the older person. The GP may refer the patient to a psychiatrist who will try to find out the cause of the depression if it is not obvious.

There are a range of approaches to treatment, including drug therapy, counselling, behaviour modification programmes (see below) and **ECT** (**electro-convulsive therapy**). An elder may be admitted to hospital so that their condition can be properly assessed. It is important to observe patients closely during the initial stages of treatment, to prevent suicide attempts.

Behaviour Modification Programme

Sometimes a person builds up unhelpful attitudes in the course of their illness which may interfere with their potential progress. An example of this might be someone who is aggressive in order to gain attention. A programme of behaviour modification might consist of carers firmly ignoring the aggressive behaviour but giving attention at other times so that only acceptable behaviour receives attention.

Carers should make sure that medication is taken and encourage a nourishing diet. Any physical condition should be treated, for example, discomforting symptoms of a chronic condition, so that the patient is as comfortable as possible. Carers should be willing to listen and encourage the older person to talk through their feelings.

Having control of your life and over decision making is vital to good mental health. Whenever possible people should be given choices and their decisions respected. Sometimes it is the loss of control which has triggered the depression in the first place and this is a preventive measure in caring for all older people.

SENILE DEMENTIA

There are two types of senile dementia; Alzheimer's disease and 'multi-infarct' dementia. Alzheimer's disease has a gradual onset and is brought about by changes in the structure of the brain resulting in greater cell death than is found in normal ageing.

Multi-infarct dementia is caused by mini-strokes occurring in the brain, resulting in small areas of dead cells. This has the effect of 'step-like' progression, where there are periods of stability then sudden deterioration. Some people suffer from both types of condition.

Dementia is a condition in which someone's intellectual ability and personality become changed and diminished. It is an extremely distressing illness which can be terrifying for sufferers, both in the early stages when it becomes apparent what is happening and later on when sufferers find themselves in a world of total confusion and helplessness.

If the onset of dementia occurs at 65 years old and over it is referred to as senile dementia and, if it occurs under 65 years old, as pre-senile dementia. It appears to affect about 6 per cent of people over the age of 65, rising to 22 per cent of people over the age of 80.

SYMPTOMS OF DEMENTIA

Memory Loss

Short-term memory loss is quite marked, and will gradually worsen as the condition progresses. In its mild form the sufferer may forget what was eaten for lunch by tea-time. Moderate sufferers may set out to do the shopping only to find on their return that they had already been out earlier that morning and the shopping is in bags on the kitchen floor. In its severest form the sufferer will not be able to remember what was said to them five minutes before.

Orientation

Orientation means being aware of time and environment. Dementia results in the loss of this awareness so that sufferers taken out of familiar surroundings will often not recall where they are. The date, month and time of day also become more difficult to remember. This factor, together with the short-term memory loss, means that sufferers will find it increasingly difficult to arrange and keep appointments and may find themselves becoming socially isolated.

Misinterpretation

Sufferers misunderstand events and their judgement of situations is impaired. Complex circumstances and concepts become impossible to fathom.

Communication

Speech may deteriorate and frustrate communication. Severe memory loss and dis-orientation compound this, making communication with the extremely demented patient almost impossible.

Personality

The personality of the sufferer changes; reactions to things which happen may be different from the usual behaviour of the elder, which is particularly upsetting for friends and relatives who know them well. Sometimes an older person may be noisy, wander or become aggressive. These marked changes in behaviour may be a legitimate response to the confused and alarming state which they find themselves in. The experience of dementia itself shatters personal confidence; the fear of getting lost or, even worse, appearing foolish, enforces a housebound existence.

Dementia is a progressive illness in which the symptoms themselves can create changes in mood and behaviour because of the sufferer's reaction to the disease process. Perversely, people with dementia have periods of lucidity, where they are aware of their predicament but are unable to do anything about it. They inhabit a world in which they become increasingly disabled by a faulty memory that leaves them finally in a state of total confusion and frustration.

It is easy to see how close family and friends are distressed by the changes of behaviour that they witness in the demented person, yet you must remember that this may also apply in reverse. The frustration and anger which carers may feel after telling their mother for the tenth time that it is three o'clock in the morning, will seem incomprehensible to someone who thinks it is time for breakfast.

If short-term memory has been reduced to losing recall of what was said five minutes ago then awareness of place, time and surroundings is also reduced to the immediate present. Sufferers are lost in this fog and even loved ones may not be recognised.

CARING FOR DEMENTIA SUFFERERS

The disease process affects people in different ways and at different rates. The important caring approach is to try and imagine how it must feel to be suffering this experience and then to consider the response for this particular person. About 80 per cent of older people with dementia are cared for at home by relatives. Often these elders have other ailments and caring may include, for example, coping with incontinence, arthritis or disability through strokes. Chapter 6 considers the help and support which is available in the local community for the family caring for someone at home.

Caring for older adults with dementia is an extremely arduous, frustrating and stressful task. As dementia affects more people in the very oldest age group, their carers will often be the 'young old', as we discussed earlier in the book. Even with full support from the medical and social services the strain can prove too much, possibly resulting in the admission of the person with dementia into residential accommodation while also severely damaging the health and morale of the carer.

As the majority of sufferers live in the community the caring approach should focus on the family unit as a whole, i.e. caring for the carers should be considered an essential part of this approach. Carers should have access to information about benefits and services, about their relative's condition and prognosis and about local self-help groups in their area, for example:

- Services, e.g. the home care service, the community nursing service (including district and psychiatric nurses).

- Benefits, e.g. income support, attendance allowance, invalid care allowance, housing benefit and special grants for home improvements and insulation.
- Voluntary groups, e.g. the Alzheimer's Disease Society, Age Concern, MIND, Caring for Carers, and Counsel and Care for the Elderly.

These are looked at in more detail in Chapter 6.

Carers may find the following suggestions useful to remember in everyday care.

- Keep life as normal as possible and work to a regular routine; it will help sufferers if life is familiar and predictable. Use memory aids, reminisce about happy times and have family photographs on view.
- Avoid confrontation if possible; rather than argue a point if the person says something silly, try instead to distract their attention away from it. Carers may be accused of stealing from the older person when they have mislaid something; this is very common and carers should try not to get upset about it.
- Keep life simple and try to prolong the sufferer's independence for as long as possible. This is good for the elder's self-esteem and keeps the workload down for carers.
- Introduce new situations, e.g. going to a day centre, gradually, in order to ease the sufferer's confusion, but new experiences should not be avoided as carers will need to take breaks to help them to cope.
- Be vigilant about safety and try to create an environment where the older person cannot endanger themselves or others. This relies on the common sense of carers, but the following aids may help: rails in the toilet and bathroom, secure floor coverings, keeping matches out of the way, switching off the gas or the cooker if the elder is left alone.
- Both carers and sufferers should try to maintain a healthy lifestyle: this includes a good diet, exercise, keeping in contact with family and friends and maintaining a sense of humour whenever possible.

CULTURE SHOCK AND THE EFFECT ON MENTAL HEALTH

Culture shock refers to the psychological effects experienced by people who settle into an environment totally different from their own. In Chapter 2 you may remember the three case studies of people who had come to this country as young adults and were now elders, and the issues this raised. They experienced culture shock when they first came to the UK but were too busy struggling to bring up families and to send money home to allow it to engulf them. People in these circumstances often promise themselves that they will eventually return home, without realising the roots that they are putting down in this country.

The generation of people from the ethnic minorities who are old now and those who are approaching retirement are likely to have been born overseas and to have come to this country as young adults. If they are now cared for by a large family network and have retired with a good pension they may have adapted to the customs of their environment. However, the evidence is that large numbers of ethnic minority elders live in inner city areas where the quality of housing is lowest and where health resources are most stretched. They were employed in low paid industries and often have little put by for retirement. Emigration often loosens family ties and leaves people separated and sometimes alone. Also, racism is an additional burden for people from ethnic minorities. Non-acceptance by the indigenous population was a source of regret for the two black elders in the case studies on pages 24–7.

Unfortunately older immigrants are especially vulnerable to mental disorders. The following situations show why an older person from an ethnic minority may be more at risk.

Communication

Although many ethnic elders are bilingual, some may have forgotten English or were not able to learn it very well. When elders do not speak English well or at all there is a major problem in all aspects of care, from correct diagnosis to providing appropriate treatment. Counselling support is not realistic through an interpreter, and not being able to read and write in English may result in a loss of benefits.

Some elders, for reasons discussed earlier, may revert back to their heritage language, which may make talking to younger family members impossible. An older person suffering from dementia will find it bewildering if everyone else is speaking a language that they do not understand.

The Experience of Women

Sometimes the women who immigrated to this country stayed at home caring for their families and had little contact with the indigenous population. They managed without learning much English and closely maintained their lifestyle mixing with their own people.

As women tend to outlive men, they can find themselves thrown into a strange and terrifying environment through the changes which old age inevitably brings, i.e. death of a spouse, hospitalisation or ill-health.

The Experience of Racism

Whether this is fear of physical abuse from strangers or rejection from neighbours or neglect from the statutory services, it is an everyday reality for black people.

If ethnic elders have these additional burdens to cope with it is not surprising that a change of environment is more traumatic for them than for indigenous older adults. If an emergency admission to hospital can cause Dora to become totally confused, imagine how much more vulnerable is the elder who speaks no English. Other difficulties may include not being able to eat the food or finding the way in which their body is handled during care both alien and distasteful.

SUPPORT FOR ETHNIC ELDERS

The access to health and social services needs to be improved for all older people, but there are certain additional measures which are specially geared to the needs of ethnic elders which could be implemented with a little imagination and understanding. The following suggestions would ease the effects of culture shock and social isolation felt by many ethnic elders:

- Culturally appropriate training for health and social service professionals who refer and assess older adults.

- An easily available multilingual interpreting service.
- Employing more bilingual and ethnic staff in order to minimise the cultural misunderstandings and communication problems in both community and residential settings.
- Flexible catering arrangements in hospitals and homes, to offer a culturally realistic choice of meals.
- Greater use of illustrations and signs in different languages in hospitals.
- Provision of clubs, day centres, homes and sheltered accommodation which cater for specific ethnic groups so that people feel more 'at home' (see Chapter 7).

ASSIGNMENT 4 | CARING FOR A CONFUSED OR DEMENTED OLDER PERSON |

The purpose of this assignment is to help you consider practical strategies for caring for confused or demented older people.

Investigate a real caring situation where a confused or demented older person is being looked after. This could be in a family home, residential accommodation or in a day centre. Write an account of the sufferer's daily living, the care they receive, any additional medical problems that they might have and a recent history of medical and social events.

Take care to respect the older person's confidentiality and seek permission of carers before you start your research. There is no need to use real names and you should not gossip about the client. It is acceptable to discuss your work with colleagues or other students in order to learn from each other.

You may like to interview the older person, carers, family members or any link workers involved with the patient. Ask them about practical problems and solutions. Ask them about their feelings, how they cope and what they do for relaxation.

Consider what particular medical and behavioural problems the patient has. How are these being tackled by carers? Have you any recommendations which you would like to make? You may also like to investigate local service provision, either that which is currently used by the older person or their carer, or any further provision which you think may be of use to them.

Summary

This chapter explored the attitudes which society holds about older people's intellects and how damaging stereotyping can be in the diagnosis, treatment and referral of elders for treatment. Age does not diminish intellectual ability.

Confusion can be caused by physical illness, medication and emotional trauma, usually involving loss or change. Treatment is related to the cause, and prevention is better than cure. The caring approach should include surrounding the elder with familiar objects, calendars and clocks; maintaining a calm and reassuring attitude, using interpreters when necessary, seeking to minimise cultural divides and using reality orientation therapy.

Depression can be mild, moderate or severe and treatment may include medication and counselling therapy. Prevention of depressive states in elders includes supporting older people through loss and change, giving elders time to adjust and allowing them to participate in decision making.

There are two types of senile dementia: Alzheimer's Disease and 'multi-infarct' dementia. Approach to care is similar to that offered to a confused elder. Providing 24-hour care is very stressful for relatives and so community care should include caring for the carers as well as the sufferers.

The mental health of elders who have immigrated to this country may be more vulnerable, mainly due to communication difficulties and racism. Therefore, elders from ethnic minorities may require extra care and support, e.g. flexible catering arrangements and multilingual information in institutions. Carers should receive culturally appropriate training and more bilingual and ethnic minority caring staff should be employed.

⑥ Caring in the Community

Earlier chapters looked at examples of caring in the community and referred to services, benefits and voluntary initiatives which may be suitable to support older people and their carers at home. This chapter considers what is available in greater depth and examines the interrelationships of different types of provision.

PUBLIC SECTOR CARE

When Mary Lewis (see Case Study, pages 30–1) was a child, providing care for those unable to care for themselves or their families was left to the parish, to charities and the workhouse. People often died from starvation and disease or from the dreadful conditions which existed in the workhouse. In Mary's lifetime the welfare state has gradually been created.

THE WELFARE STATE

The welfare state refers to all provision made by the government for people's needs. Several Acts of Parliament have sought to ensure a minimum standard, above the poverty line, for all the population and affects the provision of housing, education, community care, health and income.

The three most significant Acts of Parliament were passed after the end of the Second World War. They were:

- The Education Act, 1944, which introduced compulsory education for all children up to the age of 15.
- The National Health Service Act, 1948, which created the National Health Service.
- The National Assistance Act, 1948, which established the foundation of the social security system.

STATUTORY AGENCIES

The Welfare State is composed of the following agencies:

- the National Health Service (NHS)
- the Department of Health (DH)
- the Department of Social Security (DSS)
- the Social Services Department (SSD)
- the Probation Service.

Social services departments are administered by the local authority (run by the district or county council) and the NHS is administered by district and regional health authorities.

Due to the concerns of many people, both practitioners and policy makers, there was an investigation into service provision for people in the community called the Griffiths report (1988). The government responded with a White Paper called 'Caring for People'. The legislational changes which were proposed were delayed due to administrative difficulties, so it was agreed that there should be phased implementation of the White Paper over a period of years.

Some key elements of the proposals which may affect older people are as follows:

- Local authorities will take a greater role in assessing individual needs and designing care plans.
- Local authorities will publish their plans for the development of services and make the best use of the independent sector.
- Local authorities will be responsible for the financial support of people in residential accommodation and nursing homes; they are entitled to an applicant's Income Support and Housing Benefit to go towards the cost of this provision.
- Inspection units will be established by local authorities which are responsible for checking and maintaining standards in all residential accommodation. These are independent from the management of local authority homes.
- The local authority will offer more culturally appropriate services and work more closely with members of the ethnic minority communities to do this.
- A case manager may be appointed to design a package of services for individual clients and their carers, assessing and evaluating their usefulness and effectiveness.

The changes proposed by the White Paper seek to create a more consumer-led provision by giving clients more choice, supporting local schemes, offering greater practical help to family carers, involving more people in the community, e.g. neighbours, and paying them for their care. The home care service will develop its provision to accommodate these changes, so that it can be flexible and responsive to the growing demands of the varying home situations.

The central and local government services form the statutory (i.e. state) contribution to care but these are enhanced by the contributions from the voluntary and private sector.

CARE IN THE COMMUNITY

The issues of caring for people in the community, i.e. at home, or in residential accommodation have been debated at length and it is generally considered better for people to remain in their own homes, retaining their independence for as long as possible, and receiving the support of local services and schemes. The assessment of the situation depends very much on the needs and circumstances of individuals.

If older people can still make decisions about their daily lives, and remain firmly in charge, possibly going to a day centre to socialise, then it is better for their self-esteem to live at home. Some of the advantages and disadvantages of caring for older people in the community are considered below.

Advantages

- Older people can remain in familiar surroundings which helps to prevent episodes of confusion.
- The sense of loss is minimised as elders keep their own familiar possessions, routines and long-established habits.
- Independence and autonomy are maintained to a point, although people may be dependent on services from the community, e.g. the district nurse.
- Carers can be supported, enabling partners, siblings and families to remain together.
- The cost to society is cheaper than residential accommodation.
- Supporting older people in their own homes reduces their anxiety and is far less stressful than moving them. Consequently they are more likely to have a better state of health which reduces their demands on services even further.

Disadvantages

- Older people may experience social isolation if living alone.
- There may be a loss of conversational skills.
- Older people are dependent on services which may not be completely reliable through the weather, industrial action or staff shortages.
- House maintenance might cause anxiety to some elders.
- Older people are at risk from cold weather; e.g. they may fall on ice, and maintaining a reasonable house temperature may be too expensive.
- Some elders may be at risk from unsafe acts (e.g. leaving the cooker on).
- Elders living alone are at risk from falling in their home and may not be able to raise the alarm.
- It places stress on carers if elders need a lot of supervision.

ROLE OF THE COMMUNITY WORKER

When caring for older people who do not have much contact with their families or do not have any relatives, carers may become a surrogate family. It is important to consider all the needs which families fulfil, particularly the intensely personal ones, such as loving someone, being interested in their life and respecting them.

Touch is a vital human need and we are touched daily when we live within a family in close physical contact with each other. It is something which can be lost when older people are living alone and have almost no physical contact with anyone. No-one can ever take the place of a family but community workers can do their best to be good substitutes. Home carers, care assistants, YTS trainees, voluntary workers and others will be in a position to offer this support.

Carers should show an interest in the person that they are caring for, taking time to ask them about their lives and to listen properly to what they are saying. An affectionate squeeze of the hand with a smiling face is as important as doing the shopping.

Photograph courtesy of Age Concern, © Honey Salvadori

Community workers can provide support for older people and their carers by:

- communicating effectively with older people, their families, and liaising with other personnel about aspects of their care
- promoting autonomy for both old people and their carers
- appreciating and respecting the cultural and class values of both clients and colleagues
- offering practical support
- providing physical care
- offering love and respect

- being aware and informed about what is available in the community for older people
- keeping the circumstances and situations of older people confidential
- being aware of health and safety and ensuring a safe environment for older people.

WELFARE STATE SERVICES

Primary Health Care

The primary health team refers to the health personnel who work in the community. Some of these professionals have been referred to in earlier chapters, but we can now consider the community health network as whole.

- *General Practitioners (GP)*. The family doctor, or GP, is often the focal point of community health care. He or she may be the first professional that an elder sees regarding a health problem. Hospital care will be arranged by the GP, as well as referrals to other practitioners such as the district nursing service, the community psychiatric service and paramedical personnel, e.g. the physiotherapist. The GP can refer patients to medical specialists and for hospital tests, e.g. X-rays and blood tests.
  The family doctor may have known the patient and their family for years and can be invaluable in assessing changes in needs and health or the support from family and friends. The GP often plays a key role in case conferences which consider the best care options for people.
- *District nursing service*. The district nursing service comprises a team of nursing personnel who will help with washing, bathing, dressing and getting someone up and putting them to bed in their own home. The district nursing sister or district charge nurse will also change dressings, give injections and advise carers and patients on nursing procedures. She or he will liaise with the family doctor about the patient's condition and may refer the patient to other caring practitioners and services, e.g. the home care service or the occupational therapist.
  The district nursing service can also provide hearing aid spares and an incontinence service which offers advice, equipment and laundering.
- *Geriatric visitor*. The geriatric visitor can offer advice on health issues, give preventive health advice and run pre-retirement classes for people approaching retirement. She or he routinely visits all patients over 65 years old following hospitalisation.
- *Practice nurses*. Practice nurses are employed by GPs to undertake routine tasks in the surgery, e.g. removing stitches, dressing minor wounds or giving injections. Practice nurses are more likely to be employed in a health centre or a group practice, where there are several GPs working together. She or he may also take on a preventive health care role, e.g. running well woman and well man clinics and taking cervical smears. In some practices the practice nurse may have a counselling role.
- *Community psychiatric nurses*. The community psychiatric nurse's role is to support people suffering from mental illness so that they can remain in their own homes rather than be admitted to hospital. She or he may be required to administer medication and to assess the mental state of patients. The

community psychiatric nurse may also liaise with and refer to appropriate personnel and organisations which can offer practical help to both patients and carers, and can be of invaluable support to older people and their carers who are coping with confusion, depression or dementia, offering a variety of behavioural strategies and counselling.

- *Dentists.* Regular dental checks are important for older people as healthy teeth and gums enable them to eat properly. Many elders have lost their own teeth and are fitted with dentures. It is still important to have dentures checked frequently as older people's gums can change, resulting in a poor fit which impedes chewing and therefore the quality of their diet. Some dentists will do home visits.

Paramedical Practitioners

- *Physiotherapists.* Physiotherapy is concerned with improving the health and function of the body through simple corrective exercises. The physiotherapist usually works in hospitals but may also work in the community. If elders need physiotherapy to help them to recover from a stroke, or in the management of a chronic illness, e.g. arthritis, they may be referred to an out patient clinic* for this treatment, or they may be treated in their own homes.

---

*An **out patient clinic** is a hospital-based clinic for non-resident patients. Patients are seen by hospital specialists for check-ups and may receive a variety of hospital treatments at the clinic.

- *Speech therapists.* The speech therapist works with people who have difficulty in speaking. She or he works in hospitals and in clinics in the community. Older people in the community may be referred to a speech therapist if their speech has been affected by a stroke.
- *Occupational therapists.* Occupational therapy is concerned with rehabilitation and often involves teaching people how to re-learn basic living skills, e.g. dressing, washing, cooking and light household tasks. In hospitals there is often an occupational therapy department and an area in which people can practise living skills. Elders may need this support following a stroke or any other disabling condition.
  Occupational therapists have another role in the community: the assessment of people's disabilities and their living accommodation, for the purpose of providing aids that will maintain and promote their independence. In this role they often work for the social services, offering advice on the provision of handrails, lifts, kitchen apparatus, beds, hoists and anything which can make life easier and more autonomous for both older adults and their carers.
- *Chiropodist.* Chiropody is an essential service for older people who need healthy, pain-free feet in order to remain active and independent. This service is provided by health clinics and chiropodists will visit housebound elders in their homes.

Holistic Medicine

There are other approaches to health apart from the traditional Westernised approach, often collectively referred to as alternative or holistic medicine. Some of these methods of treatment have arisen from traditional Eastern medicine and so some ethnic elders may be more familiar with their approach to health care. Indigenous elders who have tried Westernised medicine and found that it has little to offer in relieving or curing their chronic complaint may wish to try an alternative form of treatment.

The following are examples of alternative medicine:

- *Acupuncture.* This involves the insertion of the tips of needles into the body at various pressure points to achieve a harmonious balance in the body's energies, in order to treat various disorders.
- *Homeopathy.* This is a treatment in which small amounts of drugs are given to the patient to produce the signs and symptoms of the disease to be cured.
- *Hypnotherapy.* This treatment induces a state of deep relaxation in which the subconscious mind can be reached, and is used to ease a variety of mental and physical disorders, for example, pain relief.
- *Faith healing.* Clients are treated by faith healers laying their hands on them and healing disease or ailments through religious or spiritual powers.
- *Aromatherapy.* This is a method of treatment which uses the aroma from the essence of herbs and flowers to heal and soothe. These essential oils may be massaged into the skin.
- *Osteopathy.* This is the treatment of skeletal and muscular disorders by manipulation, massage and exercise.

There are no strict regulations covering the setting up of alternative practice so it is imperative for people to check that their practitioner is registered with the appropriate

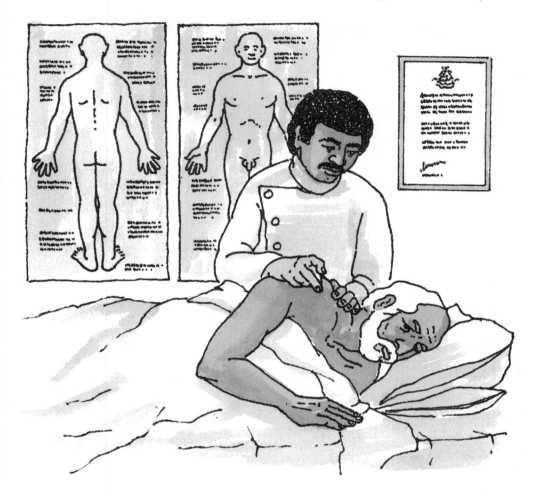

professional body. Generally speaking alternative medicine is not available on the NHS and a course of treatment can be quite expensive.

There are two main traditional Asian medical systems: the Ayurvedic and the Unanic. The Ayurvedic is basically a Hindu system whose practitioners are called Vaids. They believe that illness is caused by the elements being out of harmony in the body and prescribe treatment which may include diet, massages and herbal cures to restore balance.

The Unanic is basically a Muslim system whose practitioners are called Hakims. They believe the body has four humours which are out of balance in disease. They will prescribe massage, yoga and diet to restore health.

Asian elders may be treated by Hakims or Vaids as well as by their family doctor. This can lead to difficulties when the treatment conflicts and it would be helpful for people to explain to their GP that they are already receiving some treatment. Unfortunately some Asian elders do not speak English well enough to do this and they may also fear the disapproval of their GP.

Social Services

The role of the Social Service department is to support and enable people to care for themselves and their families. It is there to provide a social care network that will prevent people suffering deprivation when changing circumstances result in temporary or permanent hardship.

Social Services provide accommodation for people who cannot remain in their own homes for some reason. They also provide services and personnel who work in the community so that families can stay together and older people can continue to be at home and be independent.

Social workers are the facilitators of this caring network. Their role is to assess an elder's needs (and those of their carers) and to liaise with other professionals in order to assist people in coping with their difficulties. They have access to a wide range of resources and can arrange for day care, residential accommodation or a variety of home support workers, e.g. home carers.

They advise about benefits, grants and other facilities, and help with form-filling and practical matters in order to ensure that people receive the financial benefits and appropriate services to which they are entitled.

Home Care Services

- *Home carers.* Home carers offer a range of practical skills which enable older people to continue living at home. They will do housework, cooking, shopping, collect pensions and pay bills. They will also write and post letters, wash clothes and help with personal care such as washing and dressing. They can refer elders to other agencies and arrange other services, e.g. Meals on Wheels.
  Home carers regularly visit elders in their homes and provide a cheery contact with the outside world. Having a friendly conversation is as important as keeping a house neat and tidy – sometimes more so. This service is free for those people receiving benefits on a low income. The home care organiser or social worker can advise older people and their carers about exemption from payment or reduced payment.

There may be additional home care services in your area depending on the particular needs of elders and the priorities of your local authority. These may include:

- *Hospital-based service.* A team of carers based in the hospital visit patients on the wards before they are discharged. They can arrange for a home carer to visit when the patient returns home, if this is required. The nursing staff also liaise with the district nursing service, to ensure patients are visited at home following their discharge from hospital, in order to provide a continuity of care.
- *The home warden service.* The home wardens will help elders get up in the morning, perhaps helping with washing, dressing and getting breakfast. They also perform a 'tucking-in service' at night, helping older people to get undressed and putting them to bed. In some areas this type of service is carried out by the district nursing service and auxiliary nursing staff may be employed on an evening shift.
- *The night watch service.* This service can be a life-line for carers who are caring for an older person throughout the night as well as during the day. The night

watchers come at about 9 p.m. and stay until the morning. They will perform any tasks which the relatives normally have to do for their elder, leaving the family free to have a good night's sleep. The people who might benefit from this service are those caring for someone who wanders at night or who needs toileting or frequent basic nursing care. The service may be suitable for an older person living alone following recent discharge from hospital.

Other Services

- *Meals on Wheels*. This service is valuable for older adults living alone for two main reasons:
  1 A daily hot meal is delivered to an older person's home, ensuring that they have one good well-balanced meal a day. When people live alone the incentive to cook a meal for themselves may be lost and they may neglect their diets.
  2 Elders are more susceptible to hypothermia and this is one protective measure against such an occurrence. The daily visit of another person provides human contact for those who live alone and is useful for checking that all is well.
  Some areas cater for a range of diets, including diabetic, vegetarian, low fat, high fibre, high protein and halal meat. The service is often run with the help of voluntary organisations. You might like to find out which ones help to run your local service and who is responsible for deciding what is provided on the menu.
- *The Piper Alarm System*. This is a communication system for frail elders who live alone. A radio pendant is worn at all times, and this is connected to a special phone system. If the person falls or needs help, and cannot get to the phone, then a press on the pendant will send an alarm call through to a central control, who will alert the wearer's relatives or GP. If no-one is available an ambulance will be called.
- *Day care centres*. Social Services day care centres are places where elders, on referral from a doctor or social worker, can spend the day with other people. Transport to and fro is provided where possible and there may be a range of activities for people to enjoy, from keep fit to bingo. A hot lunch will be served and there is often an opportunity for a bath. Problems can be discussed and staff can refer older adults to other agencies for particular difficulties. Day centres often enable elders to remain in the community for much longer than would otherwise be possible.
  Unfortunately there are insufficient places for all elders to benefit from this vital service. Day centres are often run by voluntary organisations, churches and other religious bodies in an attempt to fulfil the need which still exists, but often the demand far outstrips the supply. Voluntary day care centres vary tremendously in their provision, according to their funding. They are more likely to cater for able-bodied people because of transport problems.
  A popular service is the Luncheon Club, usually run in church halls. This has the dietary advantages of Meals on Wheels but it also provides social contact with other people.
  Sometimes ethnic elders who might benefit from these centres have been reluctant to go because they have felt isolated within the group. Very often their specific cultural needs are not catered for, either in the food served or in the activities offered. They may also experience racism from the other elders which contributes to their feelings of alienation. There are a growing number of day

Photograph courtesy of Age Concern, © Honey Salvadori

care centres which are responding to this need, offering ethnic elders a more culturally inviting environment where they can relax and feel at home.
- *Home From Home Scheme.* Within this scheme day care is given to an elder by a host family in their home. This provides older people with social contact and personal care in a homely, intimate environment. The scheme can be extended to a full-time fostering situation where an elder lives with a foster family as an alternative to residential accommodation.

Social Services recognises the crucial part that carers play in maintaining community care and in some areas provides a range of practical services to support carers, such as the night watch service (see page 98). The day centres and Home From Home Schemes may be offered to enable a carer to continue looking after an older person. This gives carers a chance to rest and have time to themselves, to go to work or to go on holiday.

There is also a Short-stay care scheme where older people can stay with a host family (as in the Home From Home Scheme) for a few weeks so that carers can have a break. The Social Services residential homes also offer this service.

PRIVATE SECTOR CARE

The contribution from the private sector in the provision of care for older people is quite considerable, particularly in the case of residential accommodation. This area of care comprises of profit-making businesses run by individuals or organisations, which are independent from the state, although they must be registered with the local social services department. The department has statutory powers to inspect establishments and to close them down if they consider the care of elders to be unsatisfactory.

VOLUNTARY SECTOR CARE

The voluntary sector makes an enormous contribution to the provision of care for older people. Voluntary agencies are run by charitable or non-profit-making organisations which are independent of the state and the local authority, e.g. Age Concern, which provides a wide variety of local schemes including day centres, or CRUSE, which provides counselling support for the bereaved. The people who work for the voluntary sector are not all volunteers; some are waged, recruited by the charity to fulfil a full-time committed role within the organisation. For example, a day centre

Photograph courtesy of Age Concern, © Tony Othen

run by Age Concern may employ key workers to ensure regular commitment, continuity of care and the smooth running of the establishment. Of course, many voluntary workers give regular commitment but they do not have to. The advantage of a contract of employment is the security it gives to both the project leader and the establishment.

Unwaged people are involved with many care tasks, for example, visiting, shopping, providing meals, sitting for carers, doing housework, and helping with outings and other leisure pursuits. They also contribute to fund-raising, lobbying, organising, providing transport, administration and counselling.

Some voluntary organisations have national or international status with regional and local branches, e.g. MIND and Help the Aged. Others are much smaller and have been formed in response to a local need, e.g. the formation of a visiting service by the congregation of a local church for the house-bound elders of the parish.

Some organisations also have a role in speaking for the group that they represent and lobby parliament for their rights, e.g. the Midlands Pensioners Convention which campaigns to improve the resources available to pensioners. Other groups have a self-help function, enabling members to encourage each other and share problems and information, e.g. the Association of Stroke Clubs and the British Diabetic Association.

There are organisations with very specific functions, e.g. the Birmingham Talking Newspapers Association which provides weekly cassettes. Some organisations fulfil all these roles, e.g. the Association of Carers which seeks to support carers and also acts as a pressure group for improved state support. The Women's Royal Voluntary Service and the local Volunteer Bureau are useful organisations for active older people to join who wish to do voluntary work.

Sometimes voluntary organisations which are not solely concerned with older people may offer concessions or help, e.g. the RSPCA offers half-price treatment for pensioner's pets.

It is useful at this point to consider the work of one organisation and its role within the community.

AGE CONCERN

Age Concern England is a national organisation, with many local branches, which is concerned with research, training and lobbying. The local branches provide a wide range of services, including:

- A telephone link scheme: an older person who is housebound is telephoned daily at a pre-arranged time to check all is well and to promote social contact.
- A visiting service for old people: volunteers visit housebound elders to offer companionship and support.
- A good neighbour scheme: this involves visiting but might also include shopping or other light household tasks.
- Financial assistance, including insurances and the loan of televisions.
- Holidays for older people.
- Information and resources, including a reference library, the issue of publications and a funeral plan.

- Lunch clubs, day centres, activities clubs and drop-in centres have also been established as part of local community provision.

ACTIVITY

Find out as much as you can about the facilities and resources for older people which are available in your local area. Below is a checklist of questions for you to try to answer. If you have difficulty finding information on any specific query, leave it and go on to the next one.

Checklist of questions

1 How would you describe the area in which you live? Is it rural, suburban or in the city?

2 Find out what transport is available. Is it cheap, frequent, reliable?

3 Are there many older people living in your area? Is it a place where people come to retire?

4 Are there any ethnic minority communities living in your area? If there are, bear this in mind as you go through the checklist. Are the specific cultural requirements of ethnic elders being met by local provision?

5 What type of accommodation is common in your area? For example, are there many terraced houses, cottages, large old houses converted to flats, or three-bedroomed semis?

6 Are there any clubs for older adults? If so, find out who runs them and if there are any criteria for joining. Is it free? How often does it open? Does it provide transport?

7 Does the local library have any information which might be useful to older people? For example, is there a guide to local services or leisure activities? Does your library provide any special services for elders?

8 Is there a local community advice centre? If so, does it have much information for older people? Try to find out if many older people use the service.

9 Are there any local recreational centres? If so, do they provide any special facilities for elders?

10 Do any of the national voluntary organisations concerned with the welfare of older people, e.g. Age Concern or Help the Aged, have a branch in your area?

11 Find out what services the local Social Services department offers to older adults. Are any of the services provided as joint ventures with voluntary organisations?

12 What is the local Health Service's contribution to care?

13 Are there any self-help organisations for older people or their carers?

14 Can you find any privately-run enterprises for older people? If you can, briefly describe the service and the cost.

When you have completed your survey, you should have a clearer picture of the provision for elders in your area. Evaluate your findings and say whether you think that what you have found out so far is satisfactory for the older people in your area. If you have had difficulty in finding out information, you should evaluate this as well.

If older adults suffer from some of the conditions which we have discussed earlier in the book, such as a stroke or arthritis, they may have greater difficulty in getting access to the information than you did. Was information available in the languages of all the members of the local community? Do you have any recommendations for further study or proposals which would enhance the lives of older adults in your area?

FINANCES AND BENEFITS

PENSIONS

Whether people are on a high income or receiving unemployment benefit it is important they they should seek advice about their finances in retirement. Those people who have paid National Insurance contributions throughout their working lives will be eligible to claim a State Retirement Pension. The amount received depends on the type of National Insurance contribution paid and whether the pension is for a single person or a married couple. Some people can claim an additional pension from a pension scheme which they paid into while they were working.

INVESTMENT

People may invest their money in other ways in order to provide themselves with a nest-egg in retirement. Without extra money it is difficult to take advantage of the free time available for interesting hobbies and holidays (although it must be remembered that many facilities are free or reduced for pensioners).

Money may be invested in the following ways:
- The purchase of a large family house which can be sold for a smaller bungalow in retirement. The difference in price can be invested to provide an additional income on the interest.
- An endowment mortgage which accrues a substantial sum when the mortgage is paid.
- Stocks and shares.
- Life insurance policies which mature on retirement.
- Unit trusts, bonds and savings accounts.

The Citizens Advice Bureau or Pre-Retirement Association is able to suggest reputable financial consultants who can advise people how to best use their assets. It is, however, prudent to begin planning for retirement when people are young and able to make long-term choices about their savings and pension schemes.

There are people who have had no extra income to invest, who have struggled to bring up a family on a low income or who have suffered periods of unemployment. They may have worked for companies that did not have an additional pension scheme to the State National Insurance contributions. Women who have not worked because they were caring for their families or their parents may not have paid National Insurance contributions. Depending on their personal circumstances these people may be entitled to income support.

CLAIMING INCOME SUPPORT

Income support is a non-contributory benefit, which means that you do not have to have paid National Insurance contributions in order to qualify. The Government sets a limit for a minimum income and this ensures that everyone is entitled to receive sufficient money to provide for the basic requirements for living. People have to disclose their savings as the benefit is means-tested, i.e. those people who have some money put by (the limit is set by the government in power) will not be able to claim.

Housing Benefits

Nearly half of Britain's pensioners get help with their rent and community charge through housing benefit, paid by the Department of Social Security.

Special Grants from the Council

Housing grants are available from the council for renovating and improving property. Older people may be entitled to this, in addition to other benefits, or even if they are not receiving any benefits at all. Grants are given to provide basic amenities and repairs, e.g. an insulation grant for loft insulation to prevent heat-loss. Older people can claim up to 90 per cent of the cost of insulating their lofts with this grant.

Benefits for People with Disabilities

Benefits for people with disabilities that older adults or their carers may be able to claim include the Attendance Allowance and the Invalid Care Allowance.

- *Attendance Allowance.* This allowance is paid when people who are severely disabled, mentally or physically, need the constant attention of a carer. There are two rates, depending on whether the person needs care during the night as well as in the day-time. There is a six-month qualifying period for this allowance although the terminally ill are exempt from this.
- *Invalid Care Allowance.* If an older adult is receiving attendance allowance then the person looking after them may be entitled to Invalid Care Allowance. This may be claimed if the carer is unable to work because at least 35 hours a week is spent caring for someone. The entitlement is affected by the receipt of other social security payments and therefore not all carers are eligible.

(There are other benefits available to younger disabled people under the age of retirement which are not listed here.)

Concessions

There is a variety of concessionary rates for older people and sometimes payment is exempted altogether. For example:

(a) Men over 65 and women over 60 are entitled to
- free prescriptions
- free bus passes (not available in all areas)
- free loan of hearing aids and batteries.

(b) Those on Income Support are entitled to:
- free wigs and elastic or fabric stockings for out-patients
- free dental treatment
- free glasses
- help with fares to and from hospital.

(c) Concessionary rates are sometimes offered for:
- the theatre
- education
- different forms of travelling
- outings
- holidays
- entry to places of interest, e.g. galleries
- joining clubs and organisations.

ASSIGNMENT 5   COMMUNITY CARE

Imagine you are an older person and have lived in your own home for 50 years, raising your family in this house. You have arthritis in your hip joint which makes walking painful, particularly if you have to carry shopping. You find bathing difficult because of the pain in your hips. You are beginning to lose contact with friends as getting out to meet them becomes harder. You were widowed two years ago and live on your own. Although your grown-up children come to visit you fairly often, you feel increasingly lonely and isolated. You try hard not to get depressed, but sometimes everything seems to get on top of you and you feel there is no point in going on.

1 Imagine a social worker has called to see you. What would you like them to provide for you? Are there any services or voluntary schemes which you think might help you? Would you prefer to give up your home and go into residential accommodation? Try to give reasons for your answers, imagining what your feelings might be. How do you feel about family and friends? Would you like to have more contact?

Either
2 Follow up this activity by interviewing a social worker who visits older people and asking her opinion on your case study,

or
3 Interview an older adult who lives alone and receives support from community care workers. Ask them how they feel about their situation. Do they like being

dependent on other people? Would they prefer residential accommodation? Are they anxious about the future?

Summary

This chapter has looked at the role of the statutory, voluntary and private services involved in community care. It considered the advantages and disadvantages of community care.

The policies concerning care in the community became the subject of legislational change, in the form of the White Paper 'Caring For People' which seeks to give local authorities a greater role in designing and implementing care plans and encourages them to make the best use of the independent sector in doing so.

The role of practitioners who work in people's homes to support older people and their families was discussed. The Health Service, Social Services, private and voluntary sector play a part in enabling people to remain in their own homes. There is also a role for those who practise holistic medicine. It was demonstrated that these services can often complement each other and that practitioners from a range of disciplines may work together to provide comprehensive care and support.

Financial support in old age is also important and carers should be aware of the investments and benefits which elders and their families may be entitled to.

7 *Residential Care Provision*

In the last chapter the advantages and disadvantages of caring for people in the community were considered. This chapter explores the advantages and disadvantages of residential care.

About 3 per cent of older people aged 65–74 and 21 per cent of people aged 75 and over live in some form of hospital or residential establishment. In England, in 1988, the number of residents over 65 in registered residential homes for older and younger disabled persons was 219 175 of which:

- 97 380 were in local authority homes
- 25 633 were in voluntary homes
- 96 162 were in private homes.

RESIDENTIAL ACCOMMODATION

Reasons why people may need residential accommodation include:

- Relatives have moved away
- Confusion
- Loneliness
- Death of a spouse or sibling
- An elderly carer cannot cope any more
- Fear of attack
- Self-neglect
- Poor housing conditions
- Depression
- Dementia
- Disability
- Illness
- Family breakdown.

The table below summarises the advantages and disadvantages associated with going into residential accommodation.

Advantages	Disadvantages
• Protection from unsafe acts, crime, falls	• Loss of privacy
• Companionship	• Loss of independence
• Prevents social isolation	• Loss of, or limited, choice about what to wear, eat, when to get up and go to bed
• A warm environment	• Loss of home and familiar possessions
• Meals prepared and served	• Loss of financial autonomy
• No heavy food shopping	• Loneliness and isolation caused by class, cultural and sex differences
• No worry about paying bills, gardening or house maintenance	• Care may not always be the best as residential accommodation varies tremendously
• Peace of mind for relatives	• Stress incurred by the move may lead to confusion and exacerbate any underlying illness
• Relief for carers who could no longer cope with their elder at home.	• Expensive for society to maintain.

There are several different types of accommodation available. The choice will depend on the circumstances and dependence of the individual, the urgency of the need and the income or savings of the older person.

SHELTERED HOUSING

This is suitable for people who wish to maintain their independence but who need the extra security of someone who is easily available at all times. The type of accommodation may be a bedsitter, or small flat, a bungalow, a maisonette or even a converted tower block. It can be provided by the housing department, housing associations, social services, voluntary organisations and the private sector.

Rosie and Edward Packard (case study, page 14) live in sheltered accommodation. Can you remember what facilities are available to them? What advantages do they have over living at home? Can you think of any reasons why this arrangement might not suit everyone? Jot them down before you read on.

Advantages

- It may suit someone who is lonely and has lost a partner, family or friends through bereavement, illness or moving house.
- There is security in knowing someone will check up on you, and can come quickly in an emergency.
- Sheltered housing can provide company and an opportunity to make new friends.
- There may be help with preparing meals, laundry and cleaning (although this will depend on the establishment and its specific rules).

- There are usually opportunities to participate in leisure and recreational activities.
- Independence is maintained.
- People have a place to call their own and invite friends in for a cup of tea.
- People can have privacy when they want it.

Disadvantages

- It is a very popular form of accommodation and so places are fairly scarce. There is often a long waiting list, so people usually have to apply before they need the accommodation.
- This may mean that moving into sheltered housing is done at the convenience of the providers, not necessarily when required by the resident.
- It is not suitable for very frail, highly dependent elders.
- It may mean having to move away from a familiar locality.
- It may mean giving up a family home, and people may not be able to take many treasured possessions with them.
- It may not be a permanent move. If people become too dependent through illness or disability they will have to move out into more supportive residential accommodation.

There are some experimental sheltered housing schemes where very frail people are cared for in their own flats. These schemes have a far higher staff/client ratio than warden-managed sheltered care, and may include the following practitioners:

- a project leader, who would co-ordinate and evaluate the client's care
- a geriatric visitor
- a district nursing sister
- a physiotherapist
- care assistant staff
- domestic and catering staff.

RESIDENTIAL HOMES

Residential homes offer 24-hour care for residents and are provided by social services, voluntary organisations and private individuals. Residents may have their own rooms, or they may share. They can have help with toileting, bathing, washing, eating and dressing. Meals are usually provided in a central dining room. There is often a day room where residents can sit and watch television or mingle with other people.

Sometimes the homes are divided up into units so that residents eat and sit in smaller rooms which can be made to feel more cosy. The accommodation varies according to the structure and size of the building, the clients' needs and the care management. Recreation for residents is part of their care and should include opportunity for individual leisure as well as activities which can be shared.

Examples of recreation might be outings to the seaside or theatre, bingo, dance nights, singing round the piano, painting, keep fit, reminiscing and reality orientation therapy (see page 79). Television and radio are usually available and reading matter can be obtained through a mobile library, which will usually offer a selection of large print books if asked. Residents may be able to go out on their own or with a carer to enjoy recreation outside the home, for example, going to the pub or a local college class.

Photograph courtesy of Age Concern

SOCIAL SERVICES HOMES

Social Services Homes are sometimes referred to as 'part III accommodation'. This is because the local authority have a statutory responsibility to provide residential care for people who can no longer be supported in the community, as stated in Part III of the National Assistance Act, 1948.

The demand for these homes is great and priority is given to those in greatest need, so often the clients are very frail and highly dependent. Some Social Services homes are purpose-built and others are converted from older houses. Purpose-built homes are usually better equipped for the smaller group-living arrangements.

It is not possible to apply directly to the homes; older people need to contact their local Social Services Department. A social worker will then visit them to assess their situation.

Senior carers in local authority homes have usually had a training in care but this is more likely to be from a social work background than from nursing. Care assistants do not need formal qualifications but experience of life, and of older people in particular, is an advantage. A BTEC First Award in Care or a City and Guilds 325 in Community Care Practice would be helpful to those wishing to apply.

Photograph courtesy of Age Concern, © Nigel Dickinson

The legislation in community care outlined in the White Paper (see page 91) will make local authorities responsible for the funding of all residential accommodation. Applicants who need residential care, and who have no resources of their own, will have their costs met by the local authority who can reclaim the cost through the older person's Income Support and Housing Benefit. Local authorities will be encouraged to use the most cost-effective homes and will often place older people in a private home if it gives the best value for public money.

Private residential homes are usually run by individuals with experience in caring or in the hotel industry, but there is no legal requirement for any qualifications or specific experience. These homes must be registered with the local authority and are inspected at least once a year, but standards vary enormously.

Local authorities are now required to establish inspection units, independent from the management of their own services, which are responsible for checking the standards in all residential care establishments.

Older people and their families should shop around when looking for a suitable home. They should visit several to compare facilities and, if possible, ask for a trial stay before committing themselves. Recommendations from other people are useful in making choices. Provision of facilities varies, and what may be standard in one home is an extra in another, e.g. items such as soap or fruit. People should be advised to find out exactly what is provided for the money. Families should also enquire about flexible visiting, and ask about the supervisor's training in care.

Under the new legislation elders with no private means may have their choice restricted due to cost, although families or friends may wish to make a contribution to the cost of care, enabling them to look for a more expensive home. It is prudent to consider what facilities are wanted and what criteria are essential in choosing accommodation. The most expensive is not necessarily the best or the most suitable for someone's specific needs. For example, a small, friendly, informal home may be more cosy and flexible than a larger, less personal one.

NURSING HOMES

Nursing homes are residential homes which offer 24-hour nursing care, with a registered nurse on duty at all times. They exist in the public, private and voluntary sector. Clients are those who are too frail to be cared for in a residential home as they require more specialised nursing support. They may be bedridden following a stroke, incontinent, or require help with eating and drinking and other basic daily living activities.

HOSPITAL CARE

Sometimes older people remain as patients in long-stay wards in geriatric or psychiatric hospitals (*geriatrics* is the study and treatment of old age). The patients are dependent on nursing support and they may also be suffering from some degree of mental infirmity.

Many long-stay hospital beds for elders are in old Victorian hospitals, buildings which may have been the workhouse years ago. Some older people will remember this, perhaps increasing their anxiety about these hospitals. The wards may be 'Nightingale wards', i.e. long narrow wards with rows of beds on both sides. These conditions can make rehabilitation difficult, particularly if there is a poor patient/staff ratio and a rigid hospital routine.

Some modern hospital units are purpose-built for acute admissions, and are often geared to rehabilitation. They are usually well-resourced with nursing and other support staff, promoting an enthusiastic and positive attitude, which has resulted in the successful rehabilitation of some patients back into the community.

THE NEED FOR SPECIAL HOMES

Moving into residential accommodation is often a major upheaval for an older person who may be losing their family home and moving in with strangers. Imagine how much more difficult it would be, in addition, to face a complete change of diet, or no provision for following your religious beliefs.

If a resident is in a minority within the home – possibly the only person from their race, religion or culture – then their needs regarding their lifestyle and culture may never be met. Sometimes when people are in a majority they see allowing other people to lead their own lifestyles as special treatment, which is unfair, as the majority are never expected to make such fundamental changes. Furthermore, ethnic elders may have to endure racist comments from some members of staff and other residents, leaving them more isolated and depressed than they would have been at home.

In a truly integrated home, where the numbers of people from different cultures are more evenly spread, compromises concerning lifestyle, diet, religious observance and recreation could be arranged to provide a friendly and welcoming environment for all people. Such an environment would be far more lively and stimulating, providing more opportunities for new experiences than often exists today in many residential homes.

Photograph courtesy of Age Concern, © Honey Salvador

There is a common opinion which suggests that ethnic elders do not need residential accommodation because they are cared for by their families. However this is not always true for a variety of reasons, as you saw in Chapter 2.

There are a few homes and sheltered housing schemes which cater specifically for people of one culture in order to provide a suitable environment for ethnic elders, but these are scarce. Some Social Services Homes have established units within their homes to cater for the specific needs of ethnic minorities. The changes envisaged by the White Paper will enable Social Services to be more flexible in supporting the needs of minority communities.

ADJUSTING TO RESIDENTIAL ACCOMMODATION

Adjusting to care in residential accommodation depends on many factors, including:

- liaison between agencies
- physical and mental capabilities of the other residents
- being fully aware of what is happening
- whether the elder is suffering from a recent loss
- degree of choice and decision making allowed
- contact with the local community
- level of dependency of the elder
- relationship with family
- health of the elder
- attitude of the staff
- staff/client ratios
- disabilities of the elder
- suitability of the home for the individual's needs
- activities provided by the home
- circumstances which have made the move necessary
- relationship with other residents
- atmosphere of the home
- flexibility of the routine
- personality and attitude of the elder.

Forward planning is essential for a smoother transition from someone's own home into accommodation, but this is not always possible. The following case study considers how someone entering residential care can adjust to their new environment, looking at the factors that can help or hinder this process.

CASE STUDY *Mrs Reynolds' experience*

Mrs Reynolds, aged 83, lived with her daughter, Mrs Smith, who worked all day. Mrs Smith was a single parent who worked to support her three children. She was becoming increasingly anxious about her mother's deteriorating physical condition and the danger of her falling while she was out at work.

Mrs Reynolds became very lonely in the daytime and found the house too crowded and noisy at night. She found herself complaining about her grandchildren, which upset her as she loved them dearly. Mrs Reynolds decided it would be better all round if she went into a local home to give her daughter and grandchildren some space, and to have companionship during the day. She was aware of the strain on her family and on her daughter in particular, and did not want to fall out with her and lose contact altogether.

She brought up the subject with her daughter who was in full agreement and secretly very relieved that the suggestion had come from her mother. They began visiting several homes in the locality and found one which they both liked. It was homely and welcoming and the staff were friendly and chatty. There were about 10 residents in the home and each had their own room. Relatives could visit at any time and Mrs Reynolds could bring any special bits and pieces with her to make her room her own.

She decided to try a trial period of two weeks to see how she got on. She was glad to know in her own mind that if she really hated it, she would not have to stay, although she knew that she would have to find somewhere for the sake of her relationship with her daughter. This is what she says about her initial feelings:

'I was very apprehensive at first, leaving behind my family and being nervous of making new friends. The residents all knew each other and I felt like an outsider. I was very homesick at first. As I began to get used to the home, I started to appreciate the companionship of the other people. Perhaps they needed time to get used to me too. Mrs Tilsley and I used to go to the same school and we remembered some of the teachers. We know a lot about this area, how it's changed, how it was in the war, you know.

I got a bit fed up and wanted to come home one night. I missed my daughter and I wanted my privacy back. But I remembered how lonely I'd felt on my own and I thought to myself – there's no pleasing you is there? Anyway I decided to stay. I know it's what my daughter wanted.'

Mrs Reynolds settled into the home very quickly. Her grandchildren visit her once a week and she goes to her daughter's for lunch on Sundays.

ACTIVITY

1 What factors made Mrs Reynolds' move into the home a successful venture?

2 Briefly describe in your own words what you think might have happened if Mrs Reynolds had not moved out of the family home.

3 What other solutions could there have been to this situation?

When you have completed these questions look at the suggested answers in Appendix 1, page 145.

If you are working in a residential home for older people ask some of the residents what their feelings were when they first came into the home. Evaluate your interviews and say whether you think the older person found it easy or hard to adjust to their changing circumstances, giving reasons for your answer. Think about how carers can help older people make this transition and ask the residents what carers did which made things easier or harder for them.

WHAT CARERS CAN DO

Before someone enters a home the transition may be eased by allowing them to participate in the decision-making process, and to have a trial period before final agreement is reached. People should also be able to keep their most treasured possessions with them.

The staff may adopt the following strategies to further ease the entry of an elder into the home:

- Continue to allow people a choice whenever possible.
- Encourage a residents' forum, where issues can be discussed and negotiated.
- Assign a key worker to have a special friendship with the new resident, who can spend extra time reassuring them and listening to their anxieties.
- Introduce them to the other residents.
- Find out about any preferences they may have regarding any aspect of their care and accommodate them as far as is practical, e.g. how they like to dress themselves, what they like to eat, when they like to take a bath, how they like to take their medicine.
- Encourage contact with family and friends from outside the home and make these people feel welcome to visit at anytime.
- If possible, allow people to keep their own care practitioners, e.g. the GP, district nurse or chiropodist, to ensure continuity of care.
- Encourage residents to go out, either on their own, with other residents or with a carer (depending on their individual needs).
- Keep a dog or cat in the home; pets can have a therapeutic effect as they provide great companionship and affection, and the stroking and fondling can be especially beneficial to residents.
- Have a flexible approach, give people time, listen to them properly, let them do as much as possible for themselves, provide a range of stimulating recreational activities, encourage regular reality orientation therapy and other group activities.

LIVING IN RESIDENTIAL ACCOMMODATION

You may have done the activities in Chapter 1 and Chapter 4 on caring (pages 10 and 56). The activity in Chapter 1 asked you to consider what 'caring' meant to you. The activity in Chapter 4 asked you to think about the everyday activities which we all need to do in order to live, for example, eating and getting dressed. You were also asked to think about needing help with these tasks and how you would feel about someone looking after you. It would be useful to look back at your work and read through what you have written. Do you want to make any changes?

It is a useful exercise for carers to think about how they would like to be looked after when they are planning care for others. It may be helpful to you when reading about the pattern of residential care which follows. Try to imagine what sort of home you would like to live in.

FULFILLING HUMAN NEEDS

Charlotte Towe, in her book *Common Human Needs*, refers to six basic human needs. These are the need to:

- make decisions
- explore and find out
- form relationships
- take risks
- take responsibility
- give as well as to receive.

Carers should be aware of these needs, particularly in a residential establishment, which may unintentionally deprive people of the opportunity to fulfil most or all of these aspects of living.

ENSURING PERSONAL HELP

Clients in residential care may need help in some of the following:

- dressing and undressing and deciding what to wear
- washing and bathing
- eating and cutting up food
- cleaning teeth or dentures
- going to the toilet, wiping bottoms and cleaning up incontinence
- walking upstairs or using a zimmer frame
- getting in and out of a chair and in and out of bed
- remembering the location of the dining room or their bedroom
- remembering people, events, dates, etc.

ACTIVITY Choose one of the aspects of care mentioned above and imagine you are the carer. Write down a description of how you would help your client to accomplish the care task. Sometimes people do not want to be washed or dressed when you want them to be. How would you handle this? If you are working in a residential home, draw on your own experience and that of other carers. This activity is most usefully done either in pairs or individually and then discussed in groups.

COPING WITH SPECIFIC TASKS

The following is an example of how you might cope with helping a resident, who is suffering from dementia, to clean their teeth.

- General strategy includes establishing a familiar routine and using a friendly, pleasant approach, emphasising the pleasant side of any care activity, for example: 'Good evening, Mrs Jones. It's time to clean your teeth now. They'll feel really clean and fresh when we're finished'.
- Try to let people do things for themselves in the way they have always done them. If this is time consuming, then try to organise your care routine to

accommodate this, rather than hurrying your clients: 'Show me how you like to clean your teeth so I can help you if you need anything'.

- You may need to take people through step by step and even demonstrate what you want them to do: 'Let's just squeeze the toothpaste/fill the denture pot. . .'.
- You may need to be practical or matter of fact, but you must not get angry or upset: 'You know it's important to clean your dentures otherwise your gums will get very sore'.
- Give people a choice about how they receive care, rather than whether they will receive it. 'Would you like me to clean your dentures for you or can you manage yourself?' is better than 'Would you like to clean your dentures now or not?'.
- Is the care task absolutely necessary? Does it have to be done now? For instance, can a bath be taken later or will a wash do instead? 'I'll come back when I've finished tucking people up, Mrs Jones, and then you can put your dentures in the pot'.

ROUTINES IN RESIDENTIAL ACCOMMODATION

People in residential care may have some decisions already made for them, due to the routine of the establishment, for example:

- set meal times
- set drink times
- set bath times (and set bath days)
- set rising and bed times
- decor and furniture of their room
- sharing a room
- medication
- recreation
- what to wear
- when to go outside.

A typical day in a home may look like this:

7.00 a.m.	Get out of bed, wash and dress with help
8.00 a.m.	Breakfast
8.30–	Sit in lounge and watch television or chat (may have a morning bath)
10.00 a.m.	Cup of tea and a biscuit
12.30 p.m.	Lunch
1.00–	Sit in lounge watching television (may have an afternoon bath)
3.00 p.m.	Cup of tea and a piece of cake.
5.30 p.m.	Evening meal
7.30 p.m.	Get ready for bed
9.00 p.m.	Bed

Toileting and medication given as directed to individuals. Services and activities during the week may include the following:

- visit from a hairdresser
- bingo session
- trolley service (often run by voluntary organisations such as the WRVS) which allows residents to spend their money on sweets, magazines or toiletries.

There may also be occasional outings to the theatre or seaside, parties and sing songs. Less than this may be offered to residents, or much more. The entertainment is dependent on the time and enthusiasm of staff.

Establishments such as the one described above have been criticised for creating institutionalisation in their clients, i.e. not allowing people to make decisions or choices so that they eventually become unable to do so, and become even more dependent on care staff.

Some homes have rigid times for residents' activities for the following reasons:

- Residents are often frail, dependent, physically disabled or mentally confused and a set timetable enables staff to give everyone adequate care, particularly if there are staff shortages.
- Caring for people who need a lot of help and who can be difficult due to their mental state can be very tiring and demanding. If staff do not get sufficient respite, they may be too worn out to provide a more imaginative care structure.
- People are sometimes wary of change and new ideas and like to do things as they have always been done.
- Homes run by people with hospital experience tend to run them on similar lines.
- If residents are allowed to do things like making tea there is a greater need for staff supervision, and there may not be sufficient staff on duty to provide this extra cover.
- In a large, communal home it is difficult to allow residents greater personal freedom because of the lack of practical facilities and risk to their safety.
- Allowing residents greater autonomy would require staff training to affect changes in caring roles. This is expensive both in the cost of providing suitable courses, but more importantly in the provision of staff cover when people are away from their posts.

There are homes which allow residents greater autonomy and personal freedom. The homes are split up into units where group living takes place. Ideally this should be in small groups of about six residents, but sometimes the groups are larger.

The living arrangements differ from the more traditional home because people are encouraged to be mutually supportive and help each other. They can choose what to wear and when to rise and go to bed. They are allowed to make light meals and cups of tea and to wash small items of clothing.

They can join in with organised activities but are encouraged to arrange their own leisure and recreation as well, for example, they may go to the local college for courses. Local community groups are sometimes made welcome, so that residents have the opportunity of meeting people who are not staff or family. Residents may become involved in the running of the home, perhaps by joining a resident's association which has a say in the decision making about the care provision in the home.

Some Social Services Homes are divided into units, with larger groups of about 15 to 20 people in each unit. The units are run half way between the more rigid style used in the traditional home and the more progressive one discussed above. Residents can move about relatively freely, but there may be times for rising and going to bed, for example. The more flexible approach to care can only be given if there is a full quota of staff and sufficient time for staff evaluation of care management. It becomes progressively more difficult to adopt if residents are very frail, suffering from dementia, and therefore more dependent.

CASE STUDY *Mrs Constable*

Mrs Constable is 70 years old and came to the UK 40 years ago. She had lived in St Kitts, a small island in the Caribbean, and was married with six children. She came to this country to find work as there was high unemployment in St Kitts at that time.

Tragically her husband died before he could join her and her children were brought up by her parents in St Kitts. She continued to work in this country so that she could send money home. Mrs Constable retired when she was 60 and has had bouts of poor health. She has suffered with a leg ulcer for 15 years and this has affected her mobility.

She began going to a day centre organised by her local church for Afro-Caribbean elders, but became increasingly debilitated by her leg ulcer. She also developed mild diabetes and

the staff at the day centre felt that she was neglecting her diet. They were concerned that she needed further care than they could provide and contacted social services.

The social worker found Mrs Constable a place in a local authority home near where she lived. It was decided that Mrs Constable would no longer attend the day centre as she had 24-hour care at the home and there was a waiting list for the day centre places.

Mrs Constable did not settle well into her new home. She did not socialise with the other residents and stayed in her room more and more. She lost her appetite and started losing weight and complained of constipation. The night staff noticed that she was waking in the early hours.

When the district nurse, who knew Mrs Constable quite well, came to dress her ulcer she asked her how she liked her new home. Mrs Constable burst into tears and said that she hated it. She was the only black person here except for a couple of care assistants and domestics, she missed her friends at the day centre and the religious comfort that she got there. She hated the food and had nothing in common with the other residents. She said she felt alone and lonely and wanted to die.

The district nurse arranged to see the GP and the social worker to see if there was any way to help ease the situation. Mrs Constable was allowed to go back to the day centre for three days a week from the home while a more suitable place was found for her.

A new unit had recently been opened in a social services home on the other side of the city which catered for Afro-Caribbean elders. Mrs Constable was asked if she would like to visit it. She reluctantly agreed to go, fully prepared to be disappointed. This is what she says about her initial reaction.

'I was pleasantly surprised when I got there. There weren't many people – about five or six – they were very kind and helpful, asking me questions, but not prying. One of them came from St Kitts and we got chatting about the old days. She had some photographs which she showed me. They said that they go out to church on Sundays in the car and I would be able to go too. There was a mutton curry and dumplings for lunch and I was invited to stay. I couldn't believe it. I just sat down and cried.'

Mrs Constable was transferred to this unit. She remained in contact with the day centre and used to spend a day a week there with her friends. All her other problems have been settled; she is sleeping better, is no longer constipated and her diabetes is stable, controlled by diet only. She still has problems with her leg ulcer, but is much happier in this smaller unit and sits in the lounge chatting instead of remaining in her room alone.

ACTIVITY

1 Comment on why you think Mrs Constable's initial move into residential accommodation was unsuccessful.

2 Why was the move into the smaller unit more likely to succeed?

3 If a unit for ethnic elders had not been available for Mrs Constable, and she had had to stay in the original home, what courses of action might you have suggested for her?

When you have completed these questions, look at the suggested answers in Appendix 1, page 146.

LEISURE AND RECREATION IN RESIDENTIAL ACCOMMODATION

The leisure activities and facilities that may be available to residents in a home are:

- radio and television
- arts and crafts
- library service
- bar
- trips and outings
- bingo
- WRVS trolley
- hairdresser
- chiropodist
- physiotherapist.

ACTIVITY Write down all the leisure and recreational activities that you have participated in during the last month. Compare your list with a colleague's.

Everyone needs to take part in leisure and recreational activities. Some of the benefits which can be gained from participating in these activities are:

- being challenged and stimulated
- exercise, keeping active
- enjoyment and laughter
- having a sense of purpose
- maintaining self-esteem
- maintaining old skills and learning new ones
- helping others
- keeping mentally alert
- meeting people.

How many of the basic human needs (see page 33) fit into this?

You do many things at college, work and at home which fulfil these needs, but as a resident in a home a lot of these activities may not be possible. Consequently leisure and recreation is even more important for residents, as they have no other means of fulfilling their needs. It is part of the duty of carers to stimulate their clients, which in turn enables clients to retain their independence and individuality, even though they are dependent on others for their basic living activities.

Summary

This chapter has looked at the factors which promote good residential care. Carers should ensure that the environment is geared towards clients' individual needs. It is important that institutions cater for each client's class, cultural, religious, disability and gender needs. Clients should not have to lose their self-identity to fit into the residential setting.

Autonomy and independence may be encouraged through flexible routines, a variety of leisure experiences and the delegation of responsibility for some tasks to clients. Carers should also be aware of the need for privacy and personal freedom, to provide challenges and stimulation for residents and to allow them to participate in decision making.

8 Coping with Dying and Bereavement

People who care for older people need to be aware of how to cope with elders who are dying and with bereaved relatives. Often young people's fear of caring for the dying is caused by anxiety over coping with death itself. Some doctors and health workers may feel a sense of helplessness because there is nothing more that they can do for the patient.

THE CARER'S ROLE

There is a lot that can be done to care for older adults while they are dying, and their families. Everyone dies; it is part of life's ongoing process, but the great sense of loss that comes with bereavement, or the fear of dying itself, must not be minimised. Carers have a definite role in this final aspect of care; to be supportive, compassionate and sensitive to the needs of the patient, and the family and friends of the patient.

PHYSICAL CARE OF THE DYING PATIENT

The physical care of an elder who is dying involves keeping them as comfortable as possible. It will depend on their condition or particular illness to some extent, but will often include:

- providing warmth and ventilation
- keeping the elder free from nausea and vomiting
- enabling them to have visitors
- ensuring sleep and rest
- eye care
- mouth care; soaking dentures overnight
- providing a nutritious diet and fluids in the form of small appetising meals
- supplying oxygen as required
- turning the patient every two hours if they are in bed
- dressing wounds as required
- providing stimulants, e.g. television or radio, as required
- keeping the elder free from pain if possible
- providing medication as prescribed
- upkeep of catheter or incontinence pads if necessary
- help with going to the toilet or using a bed pan
- help with bathing or showering, or using a bed bath
- applying creams and oils if required.

When someone who has lived a long and useful life dies their death is more acceptable than, say, the death of a child. If that death was also quick and painless relatives can be comforted by the fact that their loved one did not suffer. However, the sudden death of a partner may be difficult for an elder to come to terms with, as there was no anticipation and therefore the sense of shock is greater.

If an older person dies after a long illness there may be a sense of relief that their suffering is over, but however expected the death is, the feelings of loss will be just as severe and traumatic. For an older person the grieving process may be particularly harsh as it may require readjustment of a long-held and familiar lifestyle. People are faced with the issue of their own mortality and the prospect of a lonely future.

Caring for the dying includes caring for those close to them and supporting the bereaved after the death of the patient.

SUPPORTING PEOPLE DYING AT HOME

It is important to know what support is available for people who wish to die at home. Whether carers are working in the community or in residential accommodation, they may be asked for their advice by older adults and their relatives. Elders may wish to die at home because they can be in familiar surroundings, with more personal freedom and privacy, and they can talk with family members and friends, and spiritual advisers, without fear of interruption.

It is vital to support the relatives both practically, in the ways outlined in earlier chapters, and emotionally, by ensuring that individual needs are met by providing the appropriate services and personal help. Relatives may be under tremendous pressure coping with the impending death of their loved one and will be worried that they are unable to provide suitable nursing care.

COMMUNITY SERVICES AVAILABLE

The older person who chooses to die at home, and who requires medical and nursing care will be supported by the primary health care team (the GP and community nursing service) who will be the focal point for referral for other services which may be needed, e.g. the home care team.

Home Care Teams

Some nurses specialise in caring for the dying. They are often attached to hospices, places that care for the terminally ill (i.e. people who will die from their illness). Those who work in hospices believe in maintaining the quality of life right until the end and by controlling the physical symptoms of illness they can keep people as comfortable and as active for as long as possible.

Hospices are a voluntary service, funded by charities such as Cancer Relief. Cancer Relief was founded in 1911 by Douglas Macmillan; it has provided many in-patient units and established the Macmillan nursing service. (Some teams who are fully integrated with NHS provision receive funding from the NHS as well.)

The nurses who belong to these specialised home care teams are registered nurses who have been district nurses or health visitors and who have done a specialist nursing course on care of the dying. They assess the patient's and family's medical and

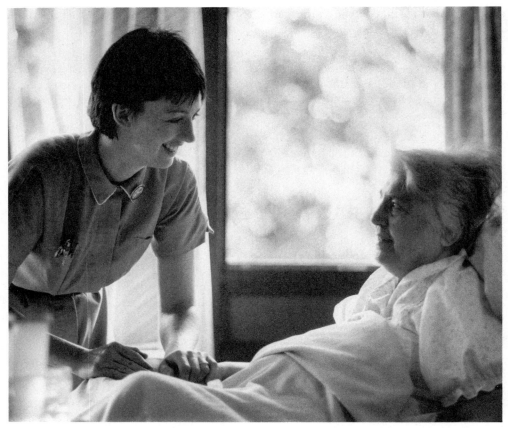

A patient receiving care in a Marie Curie nursing home. Marie Curie Centres provide cancer patients with all aspects of care, including rehabilitation, day care, terminal care and bereavement care. They provide 15 per cent of all hospice beds in the country.

Photograph courtesy of Marie Curie Cancer Care

emotional needs and offer advice on the relief of symptoms. They are also trained in bereavement counselling, continuing to advise the family after the patient's death.

The nursing care of a dying patient emphasises keeping them comfortable and helping them to maintain their independence and dignity for as long as possible. Each individual has different needs according to their illness and treatment. For example, a patient with lung disease will have difficulties with breathing and coughing and will need to be nursed sitting up. A patient who has a tumour in the stomach or digestive tract may have difficulties with eating, drinking, defaecation and may experience nausea.

The nursing staff can give advice about the appropriate care and can carry out any specialist nursing procedures. Patients requiring basic care throughout the night may receive this from a night watch service carer (see page 98), if this is available in their area, allowing the family to get some much needed sleep.

BEREAVEMENT

When people lose something or someone dear to them they experience sad feelings which express their sense of loss and this is called bereavement. They need to adjust themselves to dealing with the loss and this is the grieving process. This process consists of a series of stages which people need to work through in order to assimilate what has happened to them and to adapt to the changed circumstances of their lives.

People experience loss in varying degrees; when they lose a job or fall out with a best friend, for example, they will experience some feelings of loss. Losing a loved one through death is very traumatic as the sense of loss is severe. The need to mourn that loss is recognised in all human cultures and societies.

The length of time that people spend in each stage of grief will depend upon the circumstances of the death, the family relationships and the cultural and religious background of the person.

STAGES OF GRIEF

The Dying Person

A person may also experience the stages of grief about their own impending loss of life when they suffer from a terminal illness. It is important to be aware that an elder will go through a similar grieving process about his or her own impending death to that experienced by relatives after the death. The dying need to be given all the medical, nursing and counselling support possible.

- *Anticipation.* The grieving process starts when a person becomes increasingly poorly and begins to wonder if they will ever recover. They may ask if they are going to die – often people will ask an inexperienced carer this question, perhaps because they think they will be told the truth or, conversely, because they think that they will not. The carer, in this case, should refer them to more experienced staff. If there has been a long period of undiagnosed symptoms it may be a relief to know what is wrong. Elders know that death is inevitable and this awareness of reality can be helpful.
- *Shock.* When people first discover the truth about their condition they may suffer from feelings of shock and disbelief. They often feel totally numb, unable to take in any facts or information. They may seek a second opinion, convinced that the doctors have made a mistake.
- *Anger.* As the reality of the situation begins to dawn on them people experience a mixture of negative emotions. They may feel angry and ask 'why me?'. There will be feelings of bitterness and resentment towards the doctors and the carers and possibly family and friends too. They may become very irritable with everyone.
- *Acceptance.* Finally as the anger burns itself out the patient begins to accept the reality of the situation and may even be filled with a sense of peace and well-being. At this stage they may even be able to support their relatives and comfort them. Carers need to understand the process of an individual's need to grieve for their own impending death in order to support people and their families through this bewildering emotional crisis.

The Bereaved Relatives

- *Anticipation.* The anticipation of the death is helpful for close friends and relatives; a sudden unexpected death can be very difficult to cope with, particularly for a partner.
- *Shock.* Newly bereaved relatives may experience sensations of shock and disbelief after the death, and bereaved partners may look out for their loved one at familiar times or hear familiar noises in the house which their partner used to make. The stage of disbelief is the mind's way of coping with the shock.
- *Anger.* Gradually the reality of the death sinks in, leaving the bereaved relatives feeling angry, confused and often guilty. The feelings of guilt may be about the care they gave when the patient was ill – that perhaps it was not good enough, or that they could have done more, or about events which happened years ago, for example, a row.
  Feelings of anger towards the medical profession or family members may be expressed. There will also be feelings of bitterness against the world, and 'why me?' may be a recurring question. Sufferers may feel overwhelmed by their feelings of sadness and hopelessness.
- *Acceptance.* This is the phase of coming to terms with the loss of a loved one. Relatives may have stopped searching for their elder and have accepted that they gave the best care that they could. They may be ready to start letting go and begin adjusting to a new life. This does not mean forgetting their loved one but it does mean not living in their shadow.

SUPPORTING THE BEREAVED

Passing through these stages of grief is an active process which the patient and relatives need to work through. People do not always go through each stage and they may spend a long time in an angry phase or be unable to let go of guilt feelings. Sometimes people never reach acceptance.

It is hard to work through grief alone; the bereaved need people to listen to them talking through their feelings. This is not an easy task for family, friends and carers. It can be a very distressing and harrowing experience. It is important not to be frightened of other people's sadness. Crying is essential for people to let out their feelings and is part of the readjustment and healing process.

People sometimes avoid the bereaved because they do not know what to say to them. This can be very hurtful. It is not necessary to say anything but it is important to listen, particularly when people want to talk about their loved ones. You might say, 'I'm so sorry to hear that your husband died last week. It must be a relief that he isn't suffering any more, but I'm sure you miss him terribly'. This will allow you to express your sympathy and give the widow a chance to reply. She may well just cry. This is a natural reaction; do not feel that you have upset her. She would be more upset if no-one mentioned the death of her husband. Just sit and put an arm round her, or hold her hand, or cry with her, whatever feels right in the circumstances.

Bereaved elders may find the readjustment period particularly hard. Husbands may have had financial control of the family budget as part of their role and the newly widowed partner may need to learn new skills in money management as well as coping with her loss. Studies show, however, that women cope better with the death of a partner than men because they tend to seek the company of other widows. For some men their wife is their confidant and best friend, while women are more likely to have several close relationships with other women.

Widowers may also find domestic chores very difficult if they have never participated in the running of a home. The loneliness and practical difficulties may mean that they neglect their health. Bereavement is such a severe form of stress that it can itself be a cause of illness and even death.

Grieving for someone can take two years or longer. The bereaved often find that friends expect them to 'get over it' much sooner than this and may stop visiting or become impatient with their need to talk. Carers should be prepared to offer support for a long time and to listen and reassure whenever possible. They may be in a position to sort out practical problems, such as housing or financial difficulties, and refer the older person to someone who can help them. Voluntary organisations exist to offer support and specialist counselling for example, CRUSE, a national organisation with local branches which helps widows and widowers through skilled counselling, group meetings, etc.

The following case studies look at the care of a dying person and the family. They demonstrate the team work of different nursing personnel and the challenging task of caring for the dying.

CASE STUDY *Mr Robinson*

Mr Robinson was a retired civil servant in his early 70s, living with his wife in a suburb of Birmingham when he was diagnosed as suffering from **leukaemia***. After investigations and initial treatment in hospital it was decided that Mr Robinson would be better off continuing treatment as a hospital out-patient, and receiving care at home from the district nurse.

The district nurse found that Mrs Robinson was having difficulty in coping with the situation. She was not getting any support from her son and daughter who refused to visit their father. She could not get her husband to wash himself and he refused to let her help him. He had also become incontinent of faeces and, due to his decreasing mobility, was creating a lot of washing and soiled carpets for Mrs Robinson to clear up. He had always been a domineering person and his increasing

dependency made him irritable and stubborn. He would refuse to eat or shave, and took his frustrations out on his wife.

The district nursing team began visiting every day to provide nursing care for Mr Robinson and to offer Mrs Robinson emotional support.

Mr Robinson then suffered a relapse and his condition deteriorated. Mrs Robinson was told that his **prognosis** was very poor.

In fact Mr Robinson recovered from this and had a period of remission, i.e. a period where the symptoms of the disease subsided. The district nursing team found that Mrs Robinson took this very badly; she had been anticipating his death and had prepared herself for it. Following his improvement she became even more anxious, needing

*Medical terms printed in bold are explained in the Glossary of Medical Terms on pages 147–8.

constant reassurance that she was doing the right thing. She hardly ever went out because she felt guilty at leaving him on his own.

A Macmillan nurse also visited the Robinsons, giving support to Mrs Robinson through the last months of her husband's life. Mr Robinson's condition slowly deteriorated and he eventually died in his sleep. The district nurse and the Macmillan nurse both attended his funeral and came back to the house afterwards. Both nurses have continued to visit Mrs Robinson since the death of her husband, and her son and daughter have been much more supportive.

ACTIVITY 1

1 Imagine you are Mr Robinson. Write an account of your illness describing your feelings about your family, your care and your increasing frailty.

2 Imagine you are Mrs Robinson. Describe a day in your life during your husband's illness.

3 Imagine you are one of the nurses supporting this couple. Describe a conversation between yourself and Mrs Robinson when she needed reassuring about her husband's manner towards her.

4 Discuss your answers with others if possible.

CASE STUDY   *Mr Johnson*

Mr Johnson lived in a semi-rural town in the south of England. He was 61 years old and had taken early retirement due to ill health. He was a life-long smoker and had been diagnosed as suffering from cancer of the bronchus (a part of the lung). The Johnsons had four children, three daughters and a son.

The Macmillan nurse was informed about the patient quite early in his illness and she introduced herself to the family before she was actually needed. This helped to cement the relationship between herself and Mrs Johnson and they became quite close later on.

Mr Johnson was advised to undergo a course of **radiotherapy** as surgery was not considered appropriate treatment for his tumour. He found this rather traumatic as it left him in a lot of pain. Mrs Johnson called in the Macmillan nurse who suggested slow-release **morphine** tablets, which were pre-scribed by the family doctor. Slow-release tablets allow the drug to be absorbed into the body gradually, so that an even amount of the drug is continually working to give pain relief.

For a few weeks Mr Johnson was relatively stable. The district nurses continued to visit regularly. With his pain under control Mr Johnson was able to go to a day hospice (a day centre, usually attached to a hospice, which specialises in the care of people suffering from cancer) three times a week which he enjoyed and which gave Mrs Johnson a rest.

Unfortunately Mr Johnson's condition started to deteriorate and he became too ill to go to the day hospice. He had lost his appetite and this made his wife very anxious. She would always check with the Macmillan nurse any advice or treatment which was suggested by the district nursing team. She became extremely demanding of the Macmillan nurse's time and began ringing her day and night. Towards the end she became very irritable with the district nurses and the aids that they provided for her.

The Macmillan nurse was present when Mr Johnson died at six o'clock in the morning. She attended the funeral. She continues to visit Mrs Johnson who still needs counselling and support.

ACTIVITY

1 Mrs Johnson made increasing demands on the nursing staff, sometimes being unreasonable. Why do you think she behaved in this way?

2 How do you think carers should respond to unreasonable demands made on their time?

3 What personal qualities do you think carers need to cope with caring for dying people and their families?

Try to give reasons for your answers and discuss them with other people. If you know anyone who has experienced caring for someone who is dying, ask them if they would mind talking to you about it.

DIFFERENT CULTURAL AND RELIGIOUS APPROACHES TO DEATH

Carers may find it more difficult to care properly for dying elders who have a different cultural or religious background to themselves. Carers can be unintentionally intrusive and insensitive if they do not understand the patient's cultural patterns fully. They need to seek help to find out how best they can offer support to these elders and their families.

RESOURCES FOR SUPPORT

For ethnic elders who cannot speak English an interpreter is vital for the medical and nursing services to be effective. Often a child in the family is used but this is not satisfactory. There are many details which an older adult cannot tell a child and this may lead a misinformed carer to offer inappropriate or unsuitable treatment. It is worth making the effort to find a suitable interpreter whom the patient finds acceptable. Resources for support include the following:

- library
- spiritual and religious advisors
- interfaith organisations
- local community groups
- other carers with relevant experience
- relevant voluntary organisations
- local community worker
- the patient themselves
- the patient's family.

The following case study looks at the support the caring services were able to offer a Muslim elder.

CASE STUDY   *Mrs Begum*

Mrs Begum, a devout Muslim, lived in a large house in Manchester with her husband, grown-up children and grand-children. She had run the family shop for many years and could speak some English. A few weeks after her 60th birthday Mrs Begum discovered a lump in her breast. She did not tell anyone else about it at first, thinking that it would go away but unfortunately it seemed to get bigger. Mrs Begum started to feel more anxious about it and told her husband and eldest daughter, Yasmin.

Yasmin, a radiographer at the local hospital, was anxious for her mother to be seen by a doctor as soon as possible. The doctor examined Mrs Begum's breast and said that she needed to go into hospital very soon for a **biopsy**. Yasmin was able to help explain the procedures to her mother and interpreted some of the medical terms. The doctor was very patient and took the time to explain what would happen at the hospital and what they were looking for. Mrs Begum went into hospital three weeks later for the biopsy. Unfortunately the lump was malignant and quite far advanced. The doctors decided that a **mastectomy** was not the best course of treatment and that a combination of radiotherapy and **chemotherapy** would be more suitable.

Mrs Begum responded quite well to the treatment and the lump was reduced in size. The chemotherapy made her feel very sick despite the injections she was given to try and prevent this. She was quite well for a couple of years and spent very little time in hospital. However, around Ramadan, about three years after the lump was first discovered, Mrs Begum started to feel very weak and tired. She was getting pains in her back and arms and mentioned this at her next out-patient appointment.

She was X-rayed at the hospital, and it was confirmed that the cancer had spread into Mrs Begum's bones. They explained this to Mr Begum and Yasmin. The news was a great shock to them, even though they knew that this had been likely. However, their faith that this was Allah's will helped them and they decided to nurse Mrs Begum at home where she could die surrounded by her family.

The district nurse and family doctor came to visit Mrs Begum at home. They decided to ask for the Macmillan nurse to visit as Mrs Begum was in considerable pain and the **analgesics** which she was taking were not sufficiently effective. The men went to the Mosque several times a day to pray and they asked the Mullah to say special prayers for her.

The nurses were of white European and Afro-Caribbean ethnic origin with different religions. As part of their care, they had to appreciate the importance of Mrs Begum's place as an elder in the house and that this was seen as a family crisis rather than an individual and personal trauma for Mrs Begum. They also had to find out as much as they could about the family's religious practices so that the care that they offered would be appropriate to the family's needs. Yasmin was a tower of strength to both the family and the care workers because she was able to communicate effectively and assertively the needs of both her mother and her family. The Macmillan nurse was aware that this was putting extra stress on Yasmin, but felt inadequate to be able to offer much help.

The family were in frequent contact with their relatives in Pakistan and they turned to them for comfort and guidance. There were obvious difficulties in communication over such a vast distance and this caused problems of disappointment and indecision in the Begum household.

Finally Mrs Begum lapsed into a coma and her breathing became irregular. The family took it in turns to recite from Chapter 30 of the Qur'an. At seven o'clock in the morning Mrs Begum died. When she died they turned her body to face Mecca (which is towards the south-east in Britain). Yasmin rang the family doctor who came out to certify the death and issue the death certificate. This had to be taken to the Registrar's Office where the death was registered. The Macmillan nurse called at eight o'clock and she took out Mrs Begum's **catheter** and **syringe driver** (through which she had been receiving her pain-killing drugs). She wore gloves for this procedure in order not to defile the body. The women of the family then washed the body while Yasmin read aloud from the Qur'an. They dressed the body in a white shroud. The family had discussed the possibility of sending the body home to Pakistan for burial, but decided finally to bury Mrs Begum at the local cemetery, following the funeral ceremony at the Mosque.

The nursing staff did not attend the funeral as only men are allowed to do so, but they paid their respects at the house on the third day after the death. After a Muslim dies the family hold three memorial ceremonies on the third, the tenth and the fortieth day after the death, during which prayers are said and the Qur'an is read. These ceremonies are necessary for the dead person to be properly received by Allah.

During this period of mourning Yasmin and the other women wore plain clothes and no make-up or jewellery. Both the district nurses and the Macmillan nurse continued to visit the family during this time. They would often say 'Surely we are Allah's and to him shall we surely return', as this is a customary condolence to a relative following the death of a Muslim.

ACTIVITY 3

1 What factors helped Mrs Begum through her initial discovery of her lump, the diagnosis of her condition, her illness and her treatment?

2 Imagine that you had to go into hospital in a country where you were unable to speak the language. Would you be frightened or anxious? Write an account of your first day in hospital.

3 Discuss your feelings with others in your group.

CUSTOMS AND PRACTICES OF DIFFERENT RELIGIONS

It is not possible to give a detailed account of different religious customs in this book, but the following table offers a brief guide. It must be remembered that these are only basic details and that religious customs and practices are adapted by different families and communities and followed more strictly by some people than by others.

Religion Person Minister Holy book	Special laws	Caring for the dying patient	Laying out procedures	Funeral arrangements	Mourning period
Islam Muslim Mullah Qur'an	Five Pillars of Islam 1 Obey God (Allah) 2 Ritual washing before prayer five times a day 3 Alms giving to poor 4 Fasting at Ramadan 5 Pilgrimage to Mecca within lifetime.	Recite from Chapter 30 of the Qur'an as patient dies.	Body faced towards Mecca with head raised (south-east in Britain). Washed by Mullah or family members of same sex, not by nursing staff. Gloves worn when removing any equipment from body.	Body dressed in white. Men attend ceremony at Mosque. Condolence is said 'Surely we are Allah's and to him shall we surely return.'	Special ceremonies held on 3rd, 10th and 40th day after death, to enable soul to return to Allah. No fancy clothes, jewellery or make-up allowed until after 40th day.
Judaism Jew Rabbi Torah and Talmud	Laws for basic living: 1 Sabbath observance 2 Prayer three times a day 3 Dietary laws: Kosher meat, no pork. Jews may be orthodox (very strict), reformed or liberal.	Recite psalms, particularly the 23rd, 103rd and 139th. The Sheena is last prayer to be uttered before death. At moment of death window is opened to release the spirit.	Holy friends or Rabbi help with ritual washing of body. No post-mortem allowed unless there is a legal requirement. Candles lit and someone stays with body until funeral. Psalms are read.	Body dressed in white. Plain coffin with rope handles. Women do not usually attend funeral. No flowers. Coffin is taken past house to Chapel of Rest.	Bereaved responsible for funeral arrangements. Clothes torn at funeral symbolising grief. Seven to ten days of intense grieving, then 30 days of mourning, during which friends help with domestic duties. Candles lit and prayers said in Synagogue on anniversary of death.

Religion Person Minister Holy book	Special laws	Caring for the dying patient	Laying out procedures	Funeral arrangements	Mourning period
Hinduism Hindu Brahmin Bhagvad Gita	Belief in reincarnation and division of society into castes. Worship of Gods and Goddesses who are subordinate to a supreme being. Great reverence for all forms of life. Vegetarians.	A Brahmin blesses patient and ties thread around his or her neck. Patient should be on the floor (near to mother earth) at home. Prayers are said in special part of the house.	No special customs.	Body taken to Chapel of Rest and cremated.	Support from family, friends and Brahmin. Remembrance service each year.
Bahai Teaching from Mirza Hyssayn Ali-Iran	Believe in one God and that Jesus was a prophet. Encourage equality and adoption of a universal language.	Reciting of prayers.	Body washed and wrapped in cotton or silk shroud. Special ring placed on one finger.	Crystal, stone or fire-wood coffin. Body must be burned within one hour's journey of place where death occurred. Special prayer is read at internment.	No special customs.
Buddhism Buddhist The Sutra	Believe in meditation to improve conduct and awareness so that individuality can be lost and the soul can merge with the univer-sal life.	Supported by Buddhist monk or priest. Reciting of the Sutra. Encouraged to medi-tate and resist uncon-sciousness, remaining in a state of transcen-dency until moment of death. Patient may be shown picture of Buddha. Taking of drugs which depress the nervous system is discouraged.	No special customs.	In the West burial or cremation is accept-able, depending on family's wishes.	Funeral is considered important for bereaved to vent their grief.

Religion Person Minister Holy book	Special laws	Caring for the dying patient	Laying out procedures	Funeral arrangements	Mourning period
Sikhism Sikh Granthi Guru Granth Sahib	Five special laws: 1 Hair should be uncut 2 Comb which keeps hair in place should not be removed 3 Steel bangle should be worn on right hand 4 Short sword broach should be worn 5 Special shorts should be worn – it is offensive to remove these.	The scriptures are read. Acceptance: 'It is the will of God that we come and the will of God that we go, therefore we must accept the will of God'.	Body dressed in white.	Cremation.	Mourners dressed in white; sit cross-legged so they are not above God and do not point their feet at scriptures. Shoes should not be worn and head should be covered. Mourning period 10–13 days. Relatives feed mourners.
Chinese religions are a mixture of Confucianism and Taoism	As organised religions these are virtually non-existent but they still influence cultural behaviour. Many Chinese have fatalistic beliefs.	Family of terminally-ill patient may ask for admission to hospital so that elder's spirit will not haunt the house afterwards.	The family will help. Body dressed in new clothes for journey.	Expression of grief is encouraged at funeral. If family is small professional mourners may be employed. Paper money burnt to provide deceased with money in next life. Fire crackers used to frighten spirits away.	No special customs.

Religion Person Minister Holy book	Special laws	Caring for the dying patient	Laying out procedures	Funeral arrangements	Mourning period
Shinto (Japanese)	National religion without scriptures. Believe in Gods and Goddesses. Shinto worshippers called Tenvi Kyo practise faith healing.	No special customs.	No special customs.	No special customs.	No special customs.
The African and Afro-Caribbean experience	Believe that long-dead ancestors can communicate through dreams.	Immediately after death a bull roarer is swung to encourage spirits to beckon the dead.	Body dressed in white.	Wake for nine nights. Friends and relatives pay their respects, bring food and drink. The body is burned afterwards. Mourners leave the burial ground in different direction from that which they entered so spirit does not follow.	
Rastafarianism (founded by Ras Tafari, Emperor of Ethiopia in 1930) Rastafarian Bible and Ethiopian Orthodox Bible	Believe that Ras Tafari, known as Haile Selassie, is Messiah and will lead black people to salvation in Ethiopia. Wear natural fibres, keep their heads covered and do not cut their hair. Some are vegetarian; others do not eat pork.	Strict Rastafarians may refuse drugs (except for Ganjo which is illegal in this country). Reading prayers.	No special customs.	May adopt nine-night wake (see Afro-Caribbean experience).	
Christianity Roman Catholic Priest Bible	Believe in God the Father, Son and Holy Ghost and in the humanity and divinity of Jesus Christ.	Last rites said by a Roman Catholic Priest.	No special customs.	Burial or cremation.	Supported by family, friends and minister.

Religion Person Minister Holy book	Special laws	Caring for the dying patient	Laying out procedures	Funeral arrangements	Mourning period
Christianity Anglican Vicar Bible	Believe in God the Father, Son and Holy Ghost and in the humanity and divinity of Jesus Christ.	Patient may like to see chaplain.	No special customs.	Burial or cremation.	Supported by family, friends and minister.
Christianity Methodist Minister Bible	Teetotal.	Patient may like to see chaplain.	No special customs.	Burial or cremation.	Supported by family, friends and minister.
Jehovah's Witness Bible	No blood transfusions.	Patient may like to see minister.	No special customs.	Always takes place in a Kingdom Hall.	After initial grieving should feel positive as they will be together after the world has ended.
Mormons Bible	Believe Book of Mormons to be scriptures also.	Time for privacy and prayer twice a day.	No special customs.	Burial or cremation.	Supported by family, friends and minister.
Christian Scientist Bible	Believe disease can be healed by prayer.	Will accept treatment and may accept analgesics for severe pain.	No special customs.	Burial or cremation.	Supported by family, friends and minister.

NURSING DYING PEOPLE IN A CARE ESTABLISHMENT

Everything which has been said in this chapter applies equally to caring for the dying within a hospital or nursing home, but more care needs to be taken to provide a homely atmosphere in a care establishment, particularly if the routine of the day is rigid or if there are staff shortages.

Relatives should be encouraged to visit the patient at times convenient to them. Meals and drinks should be available for them and, if possible, a quiet room where they can have some privacy. If they wish to help in the nursing care of their elder, this should be encouraged and supported by the staff.

If an older person does not have relatives who can visit them, care staff need to be particularly sensitive and loving. If an elder has children who cannot or will not visit this will be a source of extra distress. Carers should avoid criticising the children, but should sit and listen if the person needs to talk about them.

There should be someone available to sit with the person who is dying so that they are not left alone for long periods. If this is impossible carers should pop in frequently to say a few words of comfort.

When people are close to death they often go into a coma. There is evidence that hearing is the last sense to go as people become unconscious, so it is important to talk to the dying person until they die, even if they do not respond in any way. Tell them if you are about to perform a nursing procedure and talk to them while you are sitting with them so that they know someone is there.

CARE AFTER DEATH

If an older person dies at home, the family doctor needs to be informed so that she or he can come and write out the death certificate. The time of death should be noted. The eyelids should be closed, any bags or dressings should be replaced with clean ones, dentures should be put in and the pillow should be removed, so that the head is level with the shoulders when the body starts to stiffen. The body should be covered with a sheet. Any specific religious instructions should be followed. At home the relatives may wish to sit with their loved one for a while. The undertaker will come and take the body away and will be a source of information and practical help for organising the funeral. In hospital, unless otherwise directed, or the person's religion requires a different procedure, nursing staff wash the body and dress it in a shroud. Relatives may come and sit with the patient if they wish. The body is then taken to the hospital mortuary where it is collected by the undertaker.

The important aspects of the care of dying elders and their families are:

* providing physical, practical and emotional care

- supporting the grieving process of the dying person and the family
- caring for the bereaved
- appreciating the different cultural approaches to death
- seeking resources to support the care of someone from a different culture.

This book does not contain all the information or the resources that you will need to care for elders in the community – no book could do that. It should, however, help to equip you with enough knowledge about how to approach caring situations and where to go to for help.

As a carer you should appreciate individuals, their families and their cultures as they are and seek to base the caring approach to suit the individual, rather than the other way round.

Appendix 1: Suggested Answers to Activities and Assignments

SUGGESTED ANSWER FOR ACTIVITY 3, PAGE 52

MRS SMITH'S RECOMMENDED DIETARY CHANGES

This was not a bad diet but there are some changes that could improve it. After discussion with Mrs Smith it was possible to find out what she really enjoyed and did not wish to change and what she might be persuaded to change. She loved rice pudding (which is nutritious) and her Guinness in the evening. There was no need for her to change this.

Mrs Smith's diet was low in fibre; if this could be improved her constipation may be eased. With this in mind it was suggested that she change to wholemeal bread and that she ate fruit between meals, instead of biscuits. Fruit cake is preferable to sponge cake. Mrs Smith was also willing to change her breakfast cereal. She had enjoyed porridge years ago and decided that this would make a nice change. With these alterations Mrs Smith has increased the fibre in her diet as well as the mineral and vitamin content. They are alterations which are acceptable to Mrs Smith and therefore likely to be put into practice, particularly as they should help to prevent constipation.

It was also suggested that Mrs Smith joined a luncheon club or shared some meal times with a friend so that she might rekindle her interest in food, vary her diet and enjoy the social aspects of eating again.

MR RICHARDS' RECOMMENDED DIETARY CHANGES

This diet is high in fat and sugar and by finding some alternatives the calorie content of Mr Richards' diet could easily be reduced. Mr Richards could see that his breakfast was very fattening so he agreed to have fried plantains only once a week and have cornmeal porridge in the mornings instead. He thought that he would try cutting down to one sugar in his tea or try a sugar substitute.

At lunch-time a less fattening sandwich was suggested. Mr Richards was adamant that he did not like wholemeal bread so a high-fibre white bread was suggested with a salad filling and a piece of fruit to follow.

A more nutritious alternative to fizzy pop, such as carrot juice, milk or a can of Nutriment were suggested.

It was agreed with Mr Richards that less fat in the evening meal would be preferable. Rice and peas is his favourite, but he sometimes used oil so he thought he could try it without or at least try cutting down on the amount used.

Mr Richards said he would not stop eating banana cake and having a couple of beers. Even without cutting down on alcohol the small changes made to the diet have reduced his calorie intake. Banana cake is nutritious and has a higher fibre content than most cakes, but Mr Richards was reminded that it is high in calories.

Mr Richards has replaced meals which are high in fat with high fibre, nutritious foods and as they are ones he likes he will probably keep to them. He is more conscious about using oil for cooking and may be more careful about other menus. Mr Richards is also aware that if he can lose a bit of weight it will help his arthritis and this is a great incentive.

SUGGESTED ANSWER FOR ACTIVITY 2, PAGE 73

1 MAIN CARE TASKS

The patient and his family need help with:

- communication, e.g. speech therapy with a Polish-speaking therapist
- bathing
- getting in and out of bed
- dressing and undressing
- toileting
- feeding
- mobility
- care of pressure areas
- continued physiotherapy to aid the return of function to limbs
- support for the wife as the main carer both practically and emotionally.

2 PLAN OF ACTION

Overcoming the communication difficulties by:

- seeking help from the Polish community
- involving a speech therapist
- learning key words in Polish*.

Providing physical care by:

- helping family to get patient in and out of bed and to dress, undress and bath him*
- arranging for the district nursing service to provide toileting aids*
- teaching the wife and daughter to perform basic care tasks, e.g. relieving pressure to prevent pressure sores forming and how to lift correctly
- referring family to an occupational therapist who can advise them on appropriate aids in the home
- advising on nutrition and feeding.

*indicates tasks which can be performed by an auxiliary nurse. Other aspects of the care plan would be undertaken by a district nursing sister or referred to other practitioners.

Giving practical support in the form of:

- referring family to the Social Services so that a social worker can become involved in the patient's care
- seek support for the wife from the home care and night watch service
- advise the family to contact voluntary organisations which may offer information and support, e.g. Age Concern and Association of Carers
- find a day centre place in order to relieve the pressure on the family
- find out what the Polish Community can offer.

SUGGESTED ANSWER FOR ACTIVITY 1, PAGE 81

1 WHAT HAPPENED TO DORA?

Dora became confused on admission to hospital, probably due to the shock of her physical injury, the surgery and waking up in a strange environment. The care she received, e.g. the sleeping tablets, the cot sides at night and the lack of fluids, however justified, made the situation worse. Her condition deteriorated as each health and care problem caused another to occur.

2 THE NURSING PROBLEMS

- Confusion
- Incontinence
- Awake at night
- Pressure sores
- Urinary tract infection
- Dehydration
- Infection
- Poor mobility.

3 THE CARING APPROACH

- Review medication
- Provide a nourishing diet
- Ensure a high fluid intake
- Short-term catheterisation, looking towards an effective toilet training programme
- Treatment of pressure sores (including antibiotics if necessary)
- Physiotherapy to aid mobility and prevent chest and other complications of bedrest
- Occupational therapist to assist with daily living programme
- Possible admission to rehabilitation unit with a view to returning home with community support.

Confusional states are reversible but it may be that in Dora's case there are now too many other medical and nursing problems for her to overcome in order to return to full independence.

4 PREVENTION

It would have been difficult to acclimatise Dora to the hospital as this was an emergency admission. However the care of Dora as a confused patient could have been more imaginative in order to avoid the complications that arose. The following strategies might have been implemented:

- When the sleeping tablets were proving to be ineffective at night they should have been stopped and another solution found
- Fluid intake should have been monitored immediately
- Regular toileting throughout the day and night would have prevented incontinence (catheterisation may have been appropriate post-operatively).

With these measures Dora would have been more alert in the day time and mobilisation would have been easier. If incontinence, dehydration, pressure sores and infection had been avoided then Dora's return home with support may have been possible. Once Dora was mobile, weight-bearing and free from pain, it is likely that her confused state would improve, particularly if she was allowed to return to familiar surroundings.

Sometimes staff are very much aware of the care which they should be offering but due to the fact that such a programme is so labour intensive, it is often difficult to implement it on a busy ward.

SUGGESTED ANSWER FOR ACTIVITY 1, PAGE 116

1 SUCCESS OF MRS REYNOLDS' ENTRY INTO THE HOME

Mrs Reynolds' entry into the home was quite smooth and successful, largely due to the following factors:

- It was Mrs Reynolds' own decision to move out. She was realistic about the strain she was placing on the family and on her relationship with her daughter.
- Mrs Reynolds initiated the move and was able to make choices about the most appropriate home. Although she was going into a home, she was in control of her life.
- She was able to enter the home for a trial period, knowing that if it did not work out she could move back with her daughter and look for somewhere else.
- Knowing that she was no longer a worry or a burden to her family, Mrs Reynolds could look forward to frequent visits, treats and outings.
- Mrs Reynolds' comment about the other residents needing to get used to her too is further evidence of her ability to consider the feelings of others.

2 STAYING AT HOME

- She may have fallen while her daughter was at work.
- Family tension may have increased to the point where relationships broke down irretrievably, resulting in Mrs Reynolds' entry into a home without her consultation and receiving minimal visiting from the family.
- Mrs Reynolds' daughter may have become ill through exhaustion.

3 OTHER SOLUTIONS

- Day care for Mrs Reynolds, either in a day care centre or through a Home from Home Scheme.
- Reviewing the financial situation and looking at part-time working, job sharing and entitlement to benefits.
- Asking for the assistance of a home carer, Meals on Wheels, visiting schemes and the Piper Alarm System.

SUGGESTED ANSWER FOR ACTIVITY 3, PAGE 122

1 MOVING INTO RESIDENTIAL ACCOMMODATION

Although Mrs Constable was becoming too frail to remain in the community finding her a place in a residential home was not enough. Mrs Constable had been given no choice, no trial period and had lost her only friends at the day centre. If the district nurse had not talked to her she might have remained in the home depressed and lonely. Staff who did not know her previously may not have perceived the change in her personality.

Mrs Constable felt alienated in the home because she had to change her diet and lifestyle, and had little contact with other people of her own race and culture.

2 MOVING INTO THE SMALL UNIT

By moving into the smaller unit and maintaining contact with friends at the day centre, Mrs Constable was able to maintain her cultural identity and enjoy the companionship of people who understood her.

3 STAYING IN THE ORIGINAL HOME

The solution offered by the district nurse of sending Mrs Constable to the day centre three days a week was ideal, but this might well have been reduced to one day a week due to the demand for places.

The home could possibly have made some changes to make Mrs Constable feel more welcome, for example:

- offering her food which was culturally acceptable
- enabling her to go to church on Sundays with her friends
- recruiting black care staff
- finding if any other homes in the locality had black residents and, if so, arranging for Mrs Constable to move there or at least sharing ideas with the other home for improving care
- approaching local community leaders for help in making the home more welcoming and in arranging visits from local people.

Appendix 2: Glossary of Medical Terms

acute   describes a disease or condition which is sudden, severe and of short duration.

anaemia   a condition where the quantity or quality of red blood cells in the blood is deficient, usually due to a lack of iron in the diet. Symptoms may include pale colouring of the skin and mucous membranes, tiredness and breathlessness on exertion.

analgesic   a medication which relieves pain.

artery   a blood vessel which carries blood from the heart to the capillaries.

arteriosclerosis   a condition of the arteries in which they become harder and less elastic due to the ageing process.

atherosclerosis   a condition of the arteries in which fatty deposits are laid down on the inside lining of the arteries.

atheroma   patchy degeneration in the walls of the large arteries in which fatty deposits appear.

biopsy   the removal of a tiny piece of tissue (usually undertaken as a small operation) for examination to establish diagnosis.

bronchitis   a condition in which the bronchi (the two main tubes which enter the lungs) are inflamed. This condition may be acute, caused by an infection, or chronic, caused by long term damage to the lungs.

capillary   a minute blood vessel which connects an artery to a vein.

catheter   a hollow rubber tube which is inserted into the bladder through the urethra (the part of the body through which urine is passed) in order to empty the bladder. A bag may be attached to the catheter in order to collect the urine.

chemotherapy   the treatment of disease by the administration of drugs. This is one of the methods used in the treatment of cancer.

chronic   describes a condition which is of long duration.

circulatory system   the body system consisting of the heart and blood vessels (arteries, veins and capillaries) which is responsible for circulating the blood to all parts of the body.

diffusion   the process in which dissolved substances pass across a membrane in order to establish equal amounts on both sides of that membrane.

electro-convulsive therapy (ECT)   a treatment used for some mental illnesses, usually depression, in which an electric current is passed through the frontal lobes of the brain.

embolus   a substance carried by the blood stream until it causes an obstruction by blocking a blood vessel.

emphysema   a chronic disease of the lungs in which the air sacs are enlarged and sometimes broken resulting in breathlessness, particularly on exertion.

haemorrhage   the escape of blood from its vessel.

hair follicle   the sheath in which a hair grows.

homeostasis   the process by which the body regulates and maintains its biological and chemical environment.

hormone replacement therapy   a treatment which involves giving a woman female hormones after the menopause when she has ceased to produce them herself.

hypothermia   a condition which develops when the body temperature falls below 35 degrees Centigrade (95 degrees Fahrenheit).

leukaemia   a group of diseases in which there is an abnormal increase of white cells in the blood. These diseases are 'cancers' of the blood.

malignant   a term applied to any disease which is uncontrollable and resistant to therapy, commonly used to describe cancerous tumours.

mastectomy   the surgical removal of the breast, one of a range of treatments for breast cancer.

menopause   the normal cessation of menstruation which occurs mostly between the ages of 40 to 55.

metabolism   the name given to all the chemical changes in the body, including the breakdown of substances and the creation of new material.

morphine   a narcotic drug derived from opium, used to relieve severe pain.

nephron   a microscopic, functional unit. Nephrons form the structure of the kidneys. The nephron is responsible for filtering urea from the blood and for the reabsorption of nutrients and useful substances into the blood.

neurone   a nerve cell. Neurones form the structure of the brain and nervous system. These cells co-ordinate body systems and interact with the external environment by the transmission of impulses along the cell body.

oestrogen   a female hormone produced in the ovary which plays a part in the formation of sex characteristics, in regulating menstruation and in pregnancy.

osteoarthritis   a degenerative disease which affects the joints, more usually, of older people, caused by general wear and tear over a life time. The joints which take the most weight and strain are most likely to be affected, i.e. the hips, knees and spine.

osteoporosis   a condition in which bone tissue loses mass and becomes more porous and brittle.

peristalsis   a wave-like movement in the muscle walls of tubular parts of the body which pushes the contents of that tube forward. This is the action which moves food through the digestive system.

progesterone   a female hormone which plays an important part in regulating the menstrual cycle and in pregnancy.

prognosis   the forecast of the course and duration of a disease or condition.

radiotherapy   the treatment of disease using radioactive substances. This is one of the methods used to treat malignant disease.

reality orientation therapy   a method of helping people to be in touch with what is going on around them, commonly used with older people who are suffering from dementia or loss of short-term memory.

syringe driver   a machine which is used to push a syringe filled with a drug at a slow and controlled speed, so that a patient can receive a steady dose of medication over a period of several hours.

testosterone   a male hormone produced by the testes which is responsible for the development of sex characteristics.

vein   a blood vessel which carries blood from the capillaries back to the heart.

Index

WITHDRAWN

77349